Intimacy

poems

Edited by Debra Kaufman,
Richard Krawiec,
Stephanie Levin,
and Alan Michael Parker

Cover & interior design: Daniel Krawiec

Cover image detail from:

> Alison Watt
> *Ambit,* 2011
> oil on canvas
> 60.9 x 121.9 cm
>
> Private Collection, Hong Kong
>
> Photograph: John McKenzie
> Image courtesy of the Artist and Ingleby Gallery, Edinburgh
> www.inglebygallery.com

ISBN 978-0-936481-07-4
Library of Congress Control Number: 2015949847

Jacar Press
6617 Deerview Trail
Durham, NC 27712
www.jacarpress.com

Contents

Intimacy

The Joins

*Kintsugi is the Japanese art of mending
precious pottery with gold.*

What's between us
seems flexible as the webbing
between forefinger and thumb.

Seems flexible but isn't;
what's between us
is made of clay

like any cup on the shelf.
It shatters easily. Repair
becomes the task.

We glue the wounded edges
with tentative fingers.
Scar tissue is visible history

and the cup is precious to us
because
we saved it.

In the art of *kintsugi*
a potter repairing a broken cup
would sprinkle the resin

with powdered gold.
Sometimes the joins
are so exquisite

they say the potter
may have broken the cup
just so he could mend it.

Chana Bloch

Emergent

Like wasps
stinging the unkind world
where love is stretched
and painted green
the dumb world gleaming
like bells from a tower
in a painting
of a valley, where
a single puff of steam
translates the scene.
Where to travel
on the empty train?

To sonify a spinoff,
to spin a pearl
until its oyster closes
on resistance, until
its rock finds a ready
landing in dark water,
submerging to a place
beyond eyes and the soft
underpinning of words.

In spring you want more,
the pale leaf's beckoning,
the heart's easy notice,
sky and belief
paint a notion.
The crisp, unseeming world
readies for the task.
Tell it something
it can believe.

Maxine Chernoff

The Flower and the Bone

for Georgia O'Keeffe
with whom they say
I flirted scandalously
— Frida Kahlo

Diego gave me carte blanche
with women, even encouraged me.
So why shouldn't I pursue you?
We are the same spirit
painting the flower and the bone,
the hard and the soft.
And when I fall into the mouth
of your Iris, I go moist
and remember the way
our eyes met—
if not a yes, a maybe,
don't you think.

Let me tell you Maria
was shy when she undressed for me.
She laughed like a girl,
her breasts wet clay
I spent the afternoon kneading.
And when I rolled onto her,
my breasts hung over hers,
the nipples touching
like the noses of small animals.
Then I took her into my mouth.

You're fierce as a man.
You get your way.
Your lean body says
I would like to bathe it
with my tongue.
You are the rock of the mesa
before it cools at night.
You are a pelvis opening to blue sky.

Lucinda Grey

Horses in Virginia in November

Two horses stand

side-by-side this morning in the meadow,
all sad and shiny in a hard rain, the luminous

dark planets of their eyes reminding me
grief doesn't end, but comes and goes like weather,

like the moon, like your ghost that's found
and followed me, the way the Black is always
vigilant of the shy Bay.

They need each other

like I needed you, for history and for habit,
for heart. They stand with perfect attention

while freight trains rumble down the hollow
and day hauls its winter light over them.

Sometimes the shy Bay moves off from the Black,
wanting to feel his own power, ignoring
the other's plaintive come-near neigh.

But soon they come together again.

They need each other

as touchstones, have settled between them what you
and I couldn't. Fenced by barbed wire, their lives

might seem poor and unvaried. But they have stars,
the whirling stars at night and the stars

of halved apples held out in flat palms, sweet
clover littered with diamonds, the soft-maned days.
This field is theirs,

they have each other.

Susan Elbe

The Island of Smiles

*The world once beyond the end
of my thumb...is now inside us. Everything we've lived
is now part of us...*
— Jack Myers, "Doggies' Day Out"

Candlelight fingering   our misty limbs
and you   nibbling a happy earlobe
makes our living room   a glad
sanctuary of plush red cushions.

The raspberry-scented hookah
haze   makes the air seem edible.

Your spicy tongue   rolls the hours
back to us   strolling through
Adam's Morgan   and your sly smile
when you said   *The birthday girl
gets what she wants.*

That was after fried plantains
and beef pepper stew   egusi with fish
and white rice.   It was after us
head-bobbing to bass guitars
throbbing reggae inside Bukom.

To think that finding you, and our life
as newlyweds, was once a world
that seemed beyond me—an island
of floating cabins   singing toucans
and water   so green
it emeralds in daylight.

I was a sad astronomer,
watching the sky and cursing
the improbable distance   'til a friend's
invitation to hangout   got us together
that night   shuffled in the years
stacked behind us.

If every moment we live
is now part of us,   tonight,
we're a rainy evening   and a cramped
African restaurant.

We're the storm-glazed streets
outside Bazaar Atlas—you haggling
a Moroccan merchant's price
on hand-sewn leather sandals
and sweet shisha tobacco.

We're the ride home   before
the sandalwood's burnt offering,
before the tiger's eye shimmer
on your thighs from a small flame's
broken light

Alan King

The Intimacy of Laundry

After the Ecstasy, the Laundry
— Jack Kornfield

Buzzed awake in a comfortable
        chair, I watch my husband folding
    underwear. He separates his boxers

from my underpants as if they're not allowed
        to play with each other,
    stacks the boxers in quarters, and attacks

my panties. It's one of those dry days,
        fall air full of static electricity.
    Everything he touches

crackles and jolts. My panties are loose
        and wild, flying and flinging themselves
    at him, clinging, one on each arm,

one on his chest, another grabbing
        his crotch. He peels them off,
    turns them right side out, cotton lining

demurely tucked inside. He shakes
        and smooths
    their wrinkles, builds a slippery mound

beside the tower of boxers, holds
        the last pair against his face as if
    listening to a secret, and pulls my panties

down, slowly, across his whiskery skin.
        Every cell in my body
    registers the voltage. I curse

my plain white nylon briefs,
        wish for black lace
    or some unholy shade of red.

Diane Lockward

Fever

Alone, which has grown to mean without you,
　　I sweat in our old bed. In the bay, the storm's orchestra tunes.
Thunder, and my next expression is one of yours.
　　As if in need of something lost, wind tears
through the garden. It checks all my blooms. Rain
　　falls in curtains from the roof of the porch, a thin
gap where arms could part them, hems of clattering hail.
　　Foghorns tunnel through salty haze, the full-
of-vapor sound of a vanished horizon, roaming and slow.
　　Like a conductor's elbows, the wings of a crow
rise tip to tip and hover in the naked readiness that spreads
　　from the sea, through swirling reeds, to the bed
where I ache and roll. The lilac light falls suddenly dim.
　　Blinking through sweat, I imagine: you've just left, and will come
back for me soon, a bouquet of ice in your arms.

Chloe Honum

Love Waltz with Fireworks

Seventeen minutes ago, I was in love
    with the cashier and a cinnamon pull-apart,
    seven minutes before that, it was a gray-

haired man in argyle socks, a woman
        dancing outside the bakery holding
        a cigarette and broken umbrella. The rain,

I've fallen in love with it many times,
    the fog, the frost—how it covers the clovers
    — and by clovers I mean lovers.

And now I'm thinking how much I want to rush up
        to the stranger in the plaid wool hat
        and tell him how much I love his eyes,

all those fireworks, every seventeen minutes, exploding
        in my head—you the baker, you the novelist,
        you the reader, you the homeless man on the corner

with the strong hands—I've thought about you. But
        in this world we've been taught to keep
    our emotions tight, a rubberband ball we worry

if one band loosens, the others will begin shooting off
        in so many directions. So we quiet.
    I quiet. I eat my cinnamon bread

in the bakery watching the old man still sitting
        at his table, moving his napkin as he drinks
        his small cup of coffee, and I never say,

I think you're beautiful, except in my head,
        except I decide I can't
        live this way, and walk over to him and

place my hand on his shoulder, lean in close
        and whisper, *I love your argyle socks*,
    and he grabs my hand,

the way a memory holds tight in the smallest
    corner. He smiles and says,
    I always hope someone will notice.

Kelli Russell Agodon

The Massage

After he tenderizes the tensed-up slab of meat
that is my body, pale back and paler front—
kneading, gliding, rubbing, sudden tapping,
probing forgotten levels of my tissues
and stirring the sluggish circuit of the blood
with fingers whose deep pressure pushes me
past pleasure toward the verge of agony—
the therapist concludes our hour together
at the foot of the massage table, not moving
except for his hands holding my bare feet,
steadily gripping and then releasing them
by such gradual degrees that I can't tell
when his skin actually stops touching mine,
his warm oiled palms slowly pulling away
like a fade-out at the end of a film or song
so smooth I didn't notice it happening,
a mutual tapering-off and letting-go,
a welcome vanishing into black silence,
and though still flat on my back I feel as if
I'm standing, my feet rising from the ground
reluctant to bid them farewell yet lifting
their tingling soles gently up, that final layer
of cells in body and earth intermingling
so long it's hard to believe that I'm ascending.

Michael McFee

Evensong

How does it do that, the wind, read the desire of flowers?
I swear their fragrance was the color of sunset. I am watching
the scuffed sky turn dark and remembering too many friends
who followed it into the echoes of their own words. This early
in Spring a mold has begun to betray the dogwoods. I once
believed that silence revealed something of eternity. I once
believed in the geology of the soul. Today I was astonished
at how the new redbud leaves take the shape of tiny hearts.
Even a few hummingbirds have mistaken them for flowers.
Does the night blooming cereus on my windowsill believe
it is not a cactus? Not far from here the clear cut forest has
nothing left to believe in. There is no myth we have that is
not blind to that. The birds there have no idea that we exist.
It is not enough to claim some Adam dropping his bouquet
at Eve's darkening approach. He notices a chipmunk settling
on a stump. A few fish come to the surface as if to test the air.
A mockingbird opens the petals of its wings to attract a mate
with a flash of white against the gathering dark. The heron
who has been hiding all this time slaps the air awake as if
to remind us how happy we are to be here, now, accepting what
the wind brings, and loving the unbelievable fragrance of sunsets.

Richard Jackson

Blind, She Considers Her Lover

Six blind Indians felt the elephant
and made of it six entities.
So is my love, for in the dark,
where half a marriage is spent,
you are many.

First there is that silky fringe
of frontward falling hair—
you are a horse, fetchingly groomed.
You shake your head and your forelock falls
forward, steed.

Then there are your collarbones which roll,
like the bone of shells rolled by water
collected in pebbles and driftwood and weed—
you are shells on a beach,
resting in kelp-hollows.

Then the smooth skin of your back
and chest, it sings with softness.
You are bolts and drapes of some rich fabric,
organic weave of silk to velvet—
yes, you are a draper's treasure.

Lower, there is warmth and coils, springs;
countless corkscrews of millimeter breadth.
I would guess a fine steel wool,
its gauge innumerable zeros.

The legs are sturdy, lightly forested,
surely they are lichened logs.

Yet between the moss and the steel,
the strangest skin, unlike any other,
stretched, nerve-rich, another color.
Even if I were a blind Indian I'd know it;
it is itself, it is not like another.

Susan de Sola

Caravaggio's World

I love the louche look
of Caravaggio's eros
staring at me with a wicked grin.

He rises, half out, half in
the bed, one knee bent on the edge.

So irresistible it's easy
to forget the blood, and caked
arrow heads scattered across the floor.

En garde, I warn the mirror,
and fall back into my rumpled life,

gown hiked, feelings sprawled wide,
the room splattered with moonlight.

Chiaroscuro hollows the body,
each misterioso splotch
a cave I can't wait to explore,

scavenging for the treasure,
scooping it up close—

Mine! Mine!

and so devoured.

Julie Suk

More

On Paul's Hill and in Cow Mire, the butterflies land in color-
        kisses, sputter, jump in
and out of shadows. The yellow wings look like props on the
        piper cub I built as a boy
before I gave a kiss to the girl I thought I loved. The bushes grow
        more than I can

know among my scrubs and trees. August blushes understandingly.
        I swing my arms
in the John Deere's hum, my clippers on my lap in case I need to
        cut a branch or lob the handles
to free the webs the spiders have woven since I last walked Cow
        Mire Branch. I keep my body

as if wired to wish a star would jiggle through a cloud. Shadowline:
        faded pink. It looks like
mingles of dyes the washer happed on blend-and-sink. In retrospect,
        I tear at serious-seeming
touches to miss the whole complete as what had not been torn
        exactly, as we repeat longings

without hard breathing. We lie at the end of that bed, together,
        Charm and Scrub. We never say
a word, yet see the light surround in rubs of breath in places growing
        away from grace, sinking
beauty into spare halves to shape one soul in space and move
        holdings the instant we leave

unsaid the rituals of our long embrace, joy's come-ons every time
        the morning sun washes our
faces. So take your pick. Let's say that rain is good for reveries
        awhile; the days linger:
memories turn to powder the hay we rolled in yesterday, without
        recess from the quick goodbye.

Shelby Stephenson

Even when you least expect it

I knew I'd be the only
Black poet
Before I left the house
I knew I'd be mostly invisible
While simultaneously standing out
People would smile, nod
Eat cheese and drink wine
Two poets would read
From their new books
Good poetry
But nothing would relate
To my world
Still nice to be invited
To this editor's home
To know a press had interest
In my words
A good sunny day until
I walked to my car
Saw the bearded neighbor
Standing in his yard
Staring out at the liberal
White folk
Shaking his head grimacing
At the Obama bumper stickers
As the cars pulled off
Before those eyes fell on me
His sweatshirt read
Got Gun?
Above the advertisement
For his conceal and carry class
When I told my wife about it
How it made me feel
How I wanted to walk up
Choke the shit out of him

Shout, *"Got gun for who,*
For who, muthafucka!"
She said, "*Imagine*
Being a Black woman
Seeing that, then having the bastard
Wink and smile at you."

Howard Craft

March on Washington, 50th Anniversary

Technicolor this time on TV—but look hard
among the chromatic thousands

for the ones who will forever
inescapably be black and white.

They too are marching today: men with dogs
and hoses, four little girls in a church,

that fiery bus-full of students riding
for something called freedom.

And Esther, who, on that day, would set
her ironing aside, perch on a footstool

to watch. My brother, barely eleven,
entering our small den from school,

saw her face wet and twisted. He was
scared, confused. No one

had warned him about this.
All will be better now, she said, and he,

knowing she was someone he could trust,
sat down beside her to wait.

Barbara Conrad

Staying Married

November drags her wet gray wool
scarves across the valley, drapes
a shroud of sky over bone branches,
twig claws, the last dun remnants

of shivering leaves still clinging
to their origins. How can a thing
change until it's unrecognizable?
Do you remember the verdant tips

venturing forth in April, tender explosions
suffused with tentative light?
All that budding energy untapped
and humming, sweet rage of chlorophyll

beholden to no one, our fingers
loosely entwined on the path.
We thought we were different.
We thought we were free.

Now I'll trade my truth for your fiction,
settle for some light reading
or heavy petting, carry my overload
into the underworld for winter's duration,

trajectory of the fallen—the last
of the orchard cleanup cooked down
into thick, sweet, rose-pink sauce,
no hint of tart, our bodies orbiting

the gas-blue fires, drawn inexorably
to the simmering pot, cinnamon
taste of appeasement, atonement—
what we've made of it, what we've got.

Diana Whitney

Sand Dollar Island

The sky insists that all is blue and,
        except for this sand,
it almost is.

Anchor flukes hooked,
        I let the boat back out
to keep us from stranding in the ebb.

Our bodies make sharp blue shadows.

With Katie, our niece's daughter,
we wade the clear shallows,
a tawny bottom of endless wavery rib lines.

A blue crab sculls before us.

On the dry flats,
Katie stoops to retrieve a sand dollar,
her first, wowed by the perfect flower
etched on its white shell.

Wading again, we halt
when two stingrays lift off before us,
        kite-shaped with long tails
and four-foot wings that furl,
the upsweep creating a sand cloud
to hide their escape.

We tell her about those tails,
the barbs, the venom,
tell her to scuff her feet
        when moving ahead,
and soon we flush them again,

watch their graceful winging
        in a half circle around us
like phrases of a language
we want to learn and remember.

But there's no need to memorize.
Stingrays have a life of their own.
Weeks or years from now,
        stranded indoors,
we'll stare from the living room window
not seeing November rain
falling on maritime oaks and pines
but those rays
                winging
through the clear island shallows

and a thousand miles inland,
        sooner or later,
                Katie will too.

Peter Makuck

Einstein Says

"The views of space and time which I wish to lay before you have sprung from the soil of experimental physics, and therein lies their strength. They are radical. Henceforth, space by itself, and time by itself, are doomed to fade away into mere shadows, and only a kind of union of the two will preserve an independent reality."

Our world was her skin—
the odditorium of creased lines
faint with milky perfume,
wrists as though tied with elastic,
whorls in her scalp like thumbprints, like fine galaxies,
and the soft spine of her back, the delicate fontanel
above a hint of widow's peak.
What little there was of her neck,
we kissed, we inhaled. We collected
the sweet slippery bath of her, towel damp
curls reminiscent of reliquary locks.

It was like we had the keys to a temporary place,
a private realm to holiday in for most of a year.
We measured days by inching out of the nursery,
her body finally at rest
after our hummed lyrics out of tune.
We wrote on steamed mirrors, recorded star dates
on ornamented pages of milestones.

We boxed up the infant-to-three-month clothes
and then the "up to six." September became April,
became sappy toothsome months,
followed by weeks of totter and fall.
Here I am in this moment watching stellar remnants
through a viewfinder, through laugh lines,
while I climb the elliptical.

She's all layups and pop songs now.
She's emoji texts and gym bags,
she's acai berry shampoo
and gold glitter on her lashes,
don't blink, don't blink,
I hear my own mother whisper to me.
I say there is a speck in my eye,
perhaps sprung from a planet
of temporary physics.

Kierstin Bridger

Double Aquarius

A good sign, my friend says,
to be born under the new moon, the two luminaries conjoined—
a focused sign. And the girl sleeps soundly,
as if she knows it, through rain
and the furnace humming, through the creaks
of our bed, our nightly shuffling traverses
of silvered hallway. Only her hunger
                                    wakes her—one grunt
and my nipple throbs. Barred owls hunt in the expanse
of suburban yards as she snuffles and swallows,
sucks and swallows. Yesterday, while she drowsed
                        drunk with milk,
I skimmed articles about human speech evolving from birdsong—
                                    Now, in daylight,
chickadees flit in low branches of the crepe myrtle.
She's bundled in the blanket I fold three ways
to contain her. Inside, eyes fluttering again
toward sleep, she cranes her neck
then stills. The owls are long gone with their rabbits;
last night's kitchen mouse scratches in its trap.
                        In their paper on human language structure,
the researchers found a series of complex
patterns—the Bengalese finch,
for example, loops back to previous melodies
to expand its message; the nightingale
may sing us two hundred different songs.
                        (Not to us—to who? to who?)
Twisted and restrung, sung and sung—
the noonlit yard appears dead, its brown-gray grass
stiff from another night's freeze. But the buds
cling to every branch, hard,
                        waiting to blossom. They make a sound
when they finally appear—
crying? singing? a rhythmic hum?
Whatever they say, the bees hear them, and come.

Rachel Richardson

The Hymn of Constellations

Relish whatever lingers in memory:
the 4 AM birds with their songs, stitching dreams
to the waning stars to the sea, to the fog not yet

lifted, to the green field awash in mist.
A bird's note suspends over the willows:
moves first toward warble, then arpeggio,

pitch, and tremolo. Waves toss us along.
I try to stop fighting, to just relish the cool weight
of ambiguity, mussing my hair, leaving me

restless at 3 AM in dark currents. I have no
grounding claim. I am a parcel lost
beneath clouds, toyed with by wind.

From a round cabin window, I still hear
the stitching songs of the morning birds
and pray they'll call us back to land
where waves plow against pylons.

Far from home and alone, the hymn
of constellations is my only consolation.

Currents sift claws from sand,
clownfish from coral. Something squirms.
Something swims through clean, clear.
Something eyes the depths and dives.

In the city, my footfalls on sidewalks
were so steady. How sure I was then
of my direction. Time shreds and rides like foam

atop the breakers. I dream a home I've not yet lived in:
hardwood floors and brick walls,
the elaborate trill of a bird before sunrise

and those clear notes rising
before morning becomes the only thing I wake to—
my life scrubbed dusky blue—and ends the dream
I cannot recall in the face of such light.

Sharon McDermott

I Talk to My Twin, 38 Weeks Gestation

Birth's the end of it all, you're sure.
No one has come back, you say.
You mock me for believing in life
after delivery, in mother, in love.

You have never seen or smelled her.
But I know her by heart, her heart,
bass drum surrounding our snares.
She's all around us, warm, sloshing.

You ponder the empty next.
The cord is too short, you say.
We won't be able to move.
Tiny hopes just rise and die,

and I'm a fool to think there's
anything beyond what we know.
But I know we will outgrow this
tight scrum. Light will be more

than on/off, every inch we grow
is a step closer to new splendor.
We will hear her songs unmuffled.
Life after birth will engulf, delight.

And after that, a third dimension
for the color wheel. Foreign music.
Do not rest in peace, beloved. Soar,
gambol, joke, be busy, string jewel

words, exalt, exult. Who is sure death
isn't a brighter world to emerge into?

—in honor of Elise 1958-2015

Tina Kelley

Nerves

My little sister runs towards me, two years old, tumbles on the concrete,
happy and oblivious. She gets back up, her cherry-blossom dress

swinging over her diaper, but something on my face must have
tipped her off. Something in the words: *You're okay, you're okay*

must have made her freeze, look down at the blood dripping
down her knee, before bursting into tears.

It is something like a mathematics without numbers,
the loud cries of the spine, its fiery impulses scattering

like a meteor shower across the brain. Occasionally, it comes
like a thing of beauty, with long hair and a glittery chiffon dress,

a bright aura emanating from the sky like an eternally warm bath,
seconds before a dozen trigeminal boots begin stomping their feet.

There was a time people got lobotomies to displace the nerves,
sever the circuitry leading to the brain. Sometimes it worked.

Other times the pain returned, desperate and homeless, intent
on finding yet another warm place to sleep.

And maybe the memory of pain is worse—
like the woman from Connecticut whose arm was severed.

Her husband left her three days later, and she could feel her
        wedding ring
burn a hole through her finger on the hand that was no longer there.

Even the dead can feel pain as long as the doctors keep the
        blood moving.
Somehow the nerves speak, maybe in tongues, maybe talking
        only to themselves

but enough to cause scientists to argue for anesthesia during
          organ donation.
And what are we to do? How do we survive when even the dying fail?

Sometimes, it is a matter of attention
a matter of looking away.

Take a bleeding child in your hands.
Point to the odd shaped clouds in the sky.
And wait.

Kelly Michels

My Mother Ceridwen

The light on the icon,
the way I see her in my dreams,
the core of her at the edge of darkness
in a magic cauldron always full,
never exhausted,
that brings her back to life,
guarded by a golden serpent
coiled in the shape of an egg,
the world snake marshalling
inner reserves,
the seed of a new journey,
a glimpse of a mysterious and elusive
woman in a wreath made of morning glories.
This is how she lands on the page,
slanted, looking out in space,
integrated within me
save the blue sky across her face.

Hélène Cardona

In a Small Restaurant Across from the Park

Who's to say,
in this intimate restaurant lit by licks of flame,
          where, at a corner table, candles drop flickering
                    circles onto the white linen cloths,
that it's not
a breeze from before the war that disturbs
          the molecules and their shadows, stirring to life
                    a single vibrating note at the threshold
of human hearing;
and who's to say that it's only the ambient
          street light running invisible fingers
                    over the rims of water goblets; and,
who's to say,
in the lengthening moment before she rises,
          old again from her chair on the other side
                    of the world, whose face it is she sees
before her
as pathways slide open among the years, among
          the stars, and time shivers ever so slightly
                    like a rim of finest crystal caressed,
to release
in a series of widening circles waves that will meet
          after eons of interstellar darkness, will intersect
                    as before, tremble briefly, and there,
who's to say,
might it not, at last, be safe to touch?

Marjorie Stelmach

The Healer

She lays her palms on the crown of my head
as if she is calling up strength to enter
the waste of nettles and steeps that live
in my stony skin. When she traces
its gradient, I think she can read all
that has hardened there. My spine
is a sunken tree trunk the unwary
wreck on, my shoulders a wedge of clay.
I have given myself up to this rudiment touch,
as her fingers press weighted and sure
as the bent necks of shore birds.
A scent of geraniums follows her wrists.
I want to lift out of this body,
ragged, beset. I want to grow wings.
She probes along the ribs, blades,
until slowly I begin to feel cupped, new,
not wings, but something to hold
a beginning, like a cradle
rocking in her hands,
a small boat set forth upon water.

Deborah Pope

After Surgery

I find new marks
on my body: little half moons
below my clavicles and behind my shoulders, exactly
where a man would put his hands
to draw me closer, to balance my weight
over HIS sex; three long fingernail scratches
on my thigh; another fingertip
below my left breast; the smudge of a gripping hand
behind my ankle, which was bare

when I woke up. The resident came
to my bedside, a surgeon young enough for me to be his first,
kind enough to speak my name, touch my arm
when I was still groggy—"You probably won't remember"—smile
when I smiled in response, when the post-op nurse told me

to take a deep breath. Another
nurse said the mass
clinging to the bend
between thigh and calf would be cut
from a hole behind my knee while I slept
on my back, while the surgeon lifted my ankle, while he eased
my leg up as a husband would, crooking it out of the way to penetrate
the area around the stem, the blood source, the vessels
that needed to be stopped,

while he moved
inside, while I took one deep breath after

another, while I slept,
breathing. I only remember
the mask, the anesthesiologist's face
close, the nurses, the surgeon,
the warmth of the resident's hand
on my knee, the edge of the gown
being pulled away

from my ribs, my breast exposed
for a monitor to be placed, the nurse stepping forward,
covering the darkness at the center.

Ana Garza G'z

Scars

When they were newly cut by desire,
he sat naked on the edge of the bed,
showing her every scar, turning his body
in the light of the bedside lamp—a glow
in the dark of the room that lit his face
looking down at hers upturned in awe.
The fingers-width between his brows
furrowed by a blow that had left its mark
years ago. His sweet mouth puckered
by a brutal split into perpetual kisses.
The skin of the belly, lightly furred, carved
by a surgeon, leaving a gentle smile below
the navel. That near-limp explained
by the white slash above the heel
where crashing glass had severed
the stretched cord holding his gait steady.

She wondered at the pain he had endured,
and the nature of injury and healing,
how each body bears the insignia of living—
the stories told in flesh: the fractal striations
on herself where twice the child inside
had pushed against the walls of its watery
prison, that hidden rending between her legs
through which they had torn their way out.
Those other slashes and stabs that heal
but leave tokens of a life or surgeon's knife—
the shirred stump of leg she had once seen
as her uncle moaned and felt for a limb
that had been cut away to save his life.
Or worse—the photo of a slave's back,
raised ridges spreading like a mountain
range across that atlas of human flesh.

Every wound results in some degree
of remembrance, of history. Worst
damage results in worst relic. Scars
cannot form until complete healing
occurs, she knows that now. Understands
how time itself creates the score,
knitting a blanched chain of tissue
to truss the body back together, wreathing
the tender chasm over the days and hours,
a fibrous plaiting of forged flesh. The longer
it takes, the more time, the greater the scar.
Ten years now. She still picks at that
tender place—a man with beautiful scars,
naked at her bedside—tears at
some hidden scab as the gap draws apart
once more, crimson with proud flesh.

Christina Lovin

The Bath

In the sink I wash you,
slippery as a dish,
and wrap you, kicking,
in a towel. It's you

I'll keep, and yet this pool
of shifting molecules
that holds your slough
will easily outlast
your lone configured self.

Shattered, rearranged
in aquifer and cloud,
water will stay: encased
in grass, expressed as milk
into the calf, infusing life
after life indifferently.

Why can't you, too, pass
through earth's avatars
unscathed? Must one
be tepid to endure,
partial to none?

I pat you dry and peer
into the basin, find
my features floating there
and then my arm, piercing
its own unsteady image,
reaching in to open the drain.

Joshua Coben

Positioned

My daughter skips the part where
she stands her weight on the balls of her feet
practicing relevé, goes right to her toes
in ballet flats. Through the studio's glass door
I see her skipping past the building up
of ankle, strengthening her arch so it
curves in a sickle. I see her lifting, lifting.

How can I stop her from floating away,
like my mother, who would leave this world
if given the chance? She sits by her window
waiting for her god to say time's up,
she can come home.
                              She might leave it all
at any moment—the Folgers warming,
the TiVo mid-episode, the Border Collie
howling to the postman at the door.

Practice is over, the dancers
load their duffle bags over their shoulders,
but my daughter continues solo.

How can I stop watching her?
She's rising like she's empty

of everything but light.

Stephanie Levin

Practicing to Be a Poet

My father would take me to hunt
for beer cans along back roads,
easing the truck along the shoulder
and stopping at each swatch of metal.
It didn't matter if a can was dented
or rusted, I was going for quantity,
trying to build a wall display
from floor to ceiling, like the one
in Steve Costello's basement
that he and his dad had bought
at flea markets and conventions,
an impressive display of cone tops,
flat tops, Iron City Steelers cans,
and entire Schmidt wildlife sets.

Whatever my father thought of this,
he would wait, seemingly patient,
smoking Kool after Kool, as I scrambled
around ditches, and he would admire
anything I scavenged from the weeds,
saying, "That looks like a good one,"
when I would clamber back to my seat
with yet another Stag or Hamm's or Blatz.
Steve said we were wasting our time,
that nothing collected this way had value,
and I knew he was probably right,
but as my father and I drove the berms,
with Paul Harvey on the radio
and me cantilevered out the window,
I would feel a sense of possibility
as if at any moment we might find something
rare and wondrous and worth keeping.

Joseph Mills

Junkyard Communion

Sundays my sister Karen and I'd split
bags of penny candy in the junkyard
after raiding each room of our trailer
for loose change and Pepsi cans.
Climbing through the interiors
of gutted clunkers, we declared
truces that wouldn't last the day.
Our lips puckered from flavors—
sour patch, lemonhead, warhead,
airhead, sour belt, jawbreaker—
that named the failings of our mother's men.
We suffered them then—teeth clenched
until burning gave way to no taste—
so we wouldn't suffer them later. We
were happy, sliding through shattered
windshields of Ford Pintos and station wagons,
kicking cracked molding. We peered
over the dashboard's broken panels,
through cattails and foxtail barley,
listened through insect buzz and birds
chirping from radiator grills,
to soundless engines
that would take anyone nowhere.

Linwood Rumney

Letter to Father

I have tried many times to imagine what it was like and could not. I try and try and cannot imagine what it must have been like for some scrubbed-up white man to say to you that your son, your only son, was premature, would not live, and if it lived, it would be a vegetable, or at best, severely retarded. I try to imagine what you would say to mother. I try to imagine you, shoulders fallen, preparing to walk down the hallway to see me, not yet twenty-four hours old, and not yet incubated. That's how they treated preemies back then. They left us/me/your son to die within that twenty-four hour benchmark. I did not, though a part of you did. Sometimes, I think I see the you that died in the downward cast of your eyes, the light shuffle of your feet, the way you say my name: "John - son?" always a question, the way you retreat from domestic battles with a hurried HOA-LA, HOA-LA, BU YAH JAN-LA. BU YAH JAN-LA, BI-TOE...bi-toe. ALRIGHT, ALRIGHT, DON'T TALK ABOUT IT ANYMORE. DON'T TALK ABOUT IT ANYMORE, PLEASE...please?
I cannot imagine the last time everything was all right.

I used to lie awake in bed and listen to the half-Chinese, half-English, half-audible screaming, and pretend it was not you, not mother, not anything, not me. I used to imagine that God lived on the moon casting light through my window, that I would be whisked away to lie in the soft folds of his white robe, his soft, curly brown waves of hair caressing my cheek. I could find the you that died in Heaven, and make you whole again. I could heal you, would heal you, if only you would stop long enough to listen, would lift your head up long enough to look at me.

I think I always knew you were a man/my dad/not a God. I always knew it was me who made you lock up everything vulnerable in you. We both knew it was not our fault. Yet, knowledge cannot absolve the guilt. So I grew up. I played big boy. I built up walls to the world. I was perfect. I was the strongest, non-athletic, smiling boy-man the world knew. And I knew guilt and strength and joy and pain and fear and hate and violence and silence and loyalty and love. I thought I knew you, that your respect and your love, the love of you that remained alive was enough. Enough to ward off the fears and stares and hate of the world. Enough to ward off the guilt of you, of our, no, my problem. So I blinded myself to the you that died. Buried it, and stopped looking.

Today, I saw it again: the you that died. The you that joked about getting me a mail-order bride. The you that arranged a birthday lunch with my cousin because you thought I needed someone: a surrogate dad.

I needed someone today. I needed you today. So I did it again, played boy-man. I took all the fault and fear and guilt away into myself/in myself/me/and tried to set you free, again, thinking that if I was a little stronger, everything would be OK. It was not. I was not. I needed to be the little boy today, to cry about my hopes, my fears, my dreams. I wanted to lie in your lap today, to feel your fingers caress my cheek. I needed my dad today. And I do not know how to make it OK. To tell you it is not your fault. To make you hear. It is not your fault. Can you hear me? It is not your fault. And the man I am today knows that I cannot make you whole again. My words cannot make you whole. This, only you can do. All this I know, but the little boy wants to fix everything, to make everything OK. And the man is mad because somehow he knows this cannot be. So the little boy cries. The man writes to heal himself, trying hard to make everything OK, still. Still trying hard to say I love you.

Dr. Johnson Cheu

Girls, How Hungry

Once upon the bones
  of our bare story, once
upon *Once* peeled back
  to the flesh speckled candy-peach
as mine at six,

we hid behind
  a wall, we called
it Dinner, we did not know
  it loved us
like a mother. We draped

the brick porch
  in umbrellas, clustered
them pulsing like stars. Each
  bluster and bloom
held one or two girls

furled inside, our fine hair
  misting in its dollhouse
weather, soft miniature
  squalls. Spring pressed its wrists
to our knees—our

glass-blown
  roses—our breath
tracing passwords:
  inventing the codes we'd need
to enter. Ever a border,

a threshold. Once I climbed
  out from my thin-chambered turtle heart,
its green-black spines
  bent back by wind,
to wear a skin of rain

cold as March is
  when someone's six
and, hours now, sisterless. I crossed
  worlds to stand
at your possible door—lipstick pink—

and knock. Two girls in there,
  one outside. Could have tipped
the whole thing
  with my fist. Say I was drawn
that year, etched

in charcoal thirst, dense
  as soaked chalk.
The buttons on my shirt
  were not bells or suns.
I stood telling

the secret names I knew:
  sparrow
when want flapped
  intentional wings
in my eaves,

beef stew
  still brewing
like the Afterlife
  on the far stove. And *Tillie*,
the neighbor's Irish Setter

whose fur was just not here,
  her panting imaginary
on the steps now in a cloud
  of rust-lit wishes. Dread
was my season

of wet skin, of *Let-me-in*.
  I assumed rain,
its hammer thrumming
  me still
between. Once I left a dark, dry place

to get to you,
  and girls, how hungry
I've remained: forgot
  the white plate, the salt, the meat,
even the ghost voice calling me home

Sally Rosen Kindred

For the lover who eats my poems…and all the loving in-between bites

I write for these sounds of bruised whispers. Lovely indigo painted hands. Sea-washed coral brocade covers your shuddering loveliness. I gasp for mercy. Scarred rainbows leave a trail of ladies-in-waiting. Trails of spent ripeness. Trails of skin so close I can hear it breathe bleed fruit into lush. It is an evening of breaking branches that we will bandage at sunrise. Your tongue is a beckoning forest. Star-lit. Liquid whole face conjuring a delectable pilgrimage. My hair is the only map you need. Coarse uncharted navigation deep into this tangled web of throttle rhythm infinite symphonies horizons of songs. We are tangled in binding breath to prayer. Our history of sound becomes a snare drum. A decoration of some ancestral thrust. A decoration of the summer when we were full of tongues kinky mornings. You prefer a feast of hair but I offer neck shoulders a delicacy of sleepless wrists singing ribs and dangerous unhinged ankles and feet. A smile holding seven seas and unmentionable continents. We wade through a millennium of oceans tropical spasms fierce star bursts. We have stolen this land this cocoon of earth for harvest deliverance birthing of new face new love new skin. It is not a shackled dance. It is not a voodoo hoodo dance. It is not a midnight flower we bring screaming head first into this world. It is all the voices you sewed inside my heart. It is all the nights of mothers waiting. It is all the Decembers of a son's lynching. It is all the mornings swept clean of hungry ghosts. It is all the love we can carry beneath our tongues. A tenderness so wanton it lashes petals wind the inside outside of our house. Here is the place to sow. Here is the space to scalp mercy siphon full moon mirror. We are this tangled confession. Blazing bare shadows. A treason of midriffs. Honey-laced thighs. Uncouth sighs. Neon heartbeats… and in this while it is enough to slide my fingers down into a stammering heartbeat and wait for you to become my primal scream. We breathe a soundless tsunami. We become the oak covering our windows. Our roots collapsing with thunder rising beneath masked skins and a rain that claims us.

Jaki Shelton Green

How Dreamy They Are, and Beautiful

These teenagers crossing the street.
It is June, school is out,
and if they have a destination
they do not hurry to it.
One boy drapes his arm
over his girl's slim neck.
She bears the weight lightly.
Another boy and girl swing
their hands, a small hammock.
A third boy, tossing a ball
from one hand to the other,
orbits around them.
They move as in a bubble,
creating their own climate,
oblivious to the mimosa's pink tutus.
How can I help but follow
the planet of their heavenly bodies,
the breeze of their easiness,
the music of their murmurings?

Debra Kaufman

barfly

i was just a kid in those days and he was one of the bad boys
the nuns warn you about and my old man told me stay far away
from that one but i couldn't help myself and when i saw him he
was walking up to me with his marlboros tucked under his tee-
shirt like marlon brando with those biceps and his hair smelled
of his last smoke and he kissed me one of those long kisses that
just ooze out of you and shake up your insides at the same time
but what did i know back then not enough

which is why he'll always be the one that got away

last call
a ceiling fan stirs
the tip jar

Roberta Beary

the most beautiful experience
we can have is the mysterious.
[A. Einstein: *The World as I See It*]   Majorana Harem Culture

+ **T**hreshold, trespass, boundaries, I love how you kill me Majorana, kill all women here, but I believe because I want to, because of how much I love you, how willing I am to allow you to kill me so that no other woman out here has to die; I'm out here for you Majorana, do you want me? can your tongue be a good proxy, the way you sharpen it, the way you point it like a dagger when you can't help yourself and look at me, I'm trying to be something for you to see, why do you think I hike up my skirt, this is a skirt that you like, I have nothing in my wardrobe except for clothes that you like, when I'm not in them, they still smell of me, you can take them home, and if you never wash them, the smell will only intensify, and some of that might just be your memory, you will not forget me, you will become known for killing me, your new reputation, your career focus; who wins the *Majorana Prize, the Majorana medal* this year? Can you win it yourself you own reincarnated self? Hope that your reincarnation, your effigy kill me also I will die again and again just to make that happed, yes; my own brans of witchcraft, can you blame me? I hope you win several awards, no other man has done this, you are the very first to kill me, you have an ultimate distinction, guess I've done something for you, other than love you, something you didn't even want, your hands all over me, all under this skirt that I wear exclusively for your convenience, just for you, Majorana, do you like it? this skirt I keep raising higher and higher, as if it's the flag of some damn country, *Majorana Country,* I cannot leave the grounds, my freedom expires at the gate; you've locked it, you've swallowed the keys, but never would I leave you Majorana, call it Ludlow's, call it whatever you will, doesn't change the fact that all of us belong to you, your prisoners, but I like this, Majorana, I like being your victim, if's that's all that I can be for you, then I want to be victim, if being your victim means that you will touch me, that's really what I want, and what I have to have, your touch, forget about the forensic science, apparently even if my death leads to my cremation, that you killed me still can be determined from the ashes, maybe that will be hot enough for you, I tried to be some hot stuff for you, but guess I wasn't hot enough, tried to burn your hands and maybe I still do, maybe this is the way, maybe I'm really on fire, maybe this time Majorana, maybe this time I burn you, maybe I burn a tattoo into your skin, maybe it says *Killer,* maybe your skin will haunt you, your skin so tightly against mine so that your can kill me with your hands, my throat just like holding yourself to jerk off, and I do like the feel of your hands, as long as your hands touch me, as long as my skin every centimeter has your fingerprints on it, *O Majorana, O Majorana O Majorana,* bullets of sexual innuendo, go ahead and kill me for that, you make me come just with your touch, how bronze I am and becoming bronzer as the sunset of death comes closer, here I am for you Majorana, I like for you to *touch* me and this is the only way, if you Mr. Majorana become my killer, *bronze rising* between my parted legs, you part them, *little pig, little pig, little bronze pig, may I come in?* What took you so long? I was on the verge of giving up, my legs parted, stirrups of gynecology, to let men like you, the only man I like, only man I love to have a real good look, *Dr. James Marion Sims, aka Majorana, father of modern gynecology, tested his speculum on the slave girl Anarcha,* I'm her too, take a real good look at remnants of a kingdom, straw, wood, brick, burned to death, Joan of Arc, was it hard not to have a hard-on for her, guess I envy her for that, that's what I want Majorana, you anyway I can get you, does that surprise you? You are the death of me, I love you as no woman has ever loved you and I'm prepared to die for that, kill me now Majorana, I can't stand it, then you may as well kill all of us, they all have my face, as in *The Prime of Miss Jean Brodie,* the painter paints *Jean, Jean, Jean* even when he's supposed to paint the young girl he's with, his student, I am your student Majorana, in this world with you, nothing is more definite than your hands on me to kill me, I lived for this moment, your hands on every me, every woman locked inside your grounds waiting our turn to be killed, amusement park, thrill ride into your arms; I'm in your thoughts Majorana; I'm every woman, look at each of us closely, and they all become me, every woman you kill, *Killer,* is me, you storm inside me, each thrust of the blade slices me Majorana, that sharp blade in your pants, that private geyser which you know I loved, but I love you much more than any drink, any food, any chocolate, any *Old Faithful...* much more, I love you my killer, I finally get to call you mine, and this time it's true, you are MY killer, you are mine Majorana; yes, it hurts to love you; this is how I travel, you carry this memory of killing me everywhere you go; this is how I travel, I'm with you Majorana, *nighty nite* =

Thylias Moss

The Cherries at Tiffany's

The plastic cherries
near the drug store entrance
look so real

that the clerk tells us
about the children
who come in, so taken

with what seems genuine
that they dip their hands
instinctively in the bowl,

lift their faces and hold
the dazzling fruit
to their mouths.

Such lustrous deception—
red layered upon deeper
red, occasional flecks

like sparks flaring,
the thin stem a complex
of green-woven filaments,

a fibrous braid of grass,
beckoning. Who wouldn't
be seduced by this gleam

and polish? These cherries,
small charmers, are such
cunning imposters that

even we, soft and jowly
from middle age, jaded
by a lifetime of gimmickry

and artifice, cannot resist
the impulse to reach
into the bowl and disprove

the illusion, our hopeful
fingers hungry for the small
and tender heft, the delicious

resistance of the flesh.

Nancy Carol Moody

June Visit

Wild azaleas in bloom,
heat escaping the pine straw—
and as I am about to leave, car engine
already running—my father steps to my window,
leans in and dangles before me, fresh from his garden,
the most luscious strawberry I've ever seen. And he lingers
there, grinning, unable to say what I long to hear: *For
you, sweet girl.* Or, *Come back soon, my child.*
But the words hang there before my lips:
plump, ripe, glistening.

Dannye Romine Powell

E-mail from my First Boyfriend

To learn that he remembers that trip—
Beethoven's piano in Bonn, the Kölner Dom,
with its tacky hologram postcards of Christ
on the cross, even the plates of Wurstsalat—
means his memory hasn't slammed shut
its matchbox and left me cold and unstruck.
Clearly the mind is too full, he writes.
After our break-up came law school, a wife,
three children—but even so, retreading
the Rhine last summer, he glimpsed on a hill
the restaurant where we'd eaten ourselves full.
He must have seen me again, eighteen,
blonde as the Lorelei and shattered with love.

In Hamburg, we gazed at Friedrich's great
paintings, all those ruins, waves, and moonlight,
as though the artist had painted with us in mind:
the alpine storm of our emotions, our grand
longing for the future, and the deep thrill I felt,
each night, lying in some cheap hotel room.
But my boyfriend wouldn't make love to me.
Not till marriage, he said, and I so needy.

But I'm content now to exist as reverie.
I'm squinting in the sunshine, wearing a straw hat
and a yellow and white skirt, looking as I looked
that summer years ago—eager, mistaken, open,
sated with roasted potatoes and cherry cake.

Anya Silver

Obsession

I blow out candles
to free up the stubborn moon,
enmeshed in cloud.

When at last its face
blossoms beyond the trees,
blowsy-headed dahlia
spilling mist like pollen,
I thread my way through limbs
twisting into the surge of light,
spread my hands to catch the moon
in a net of words.

Branch by branch, the moon moves
upward, brushing over me
its choreography of shadows.

How can a husband sleep when the moon is up,
when it stalks through night into the balk of trees?
How, in this mythology, is he not swept awake
to plunge into the storm of light with me?

Susan Lefler

Your Secret Life

Now that you are married
you never speak of it.
When a friend asks you if
you saw a movie, you don't tell her,
We undressed before
the mirror, I let my hair down
and saw the color of his hands
against my breasts.

You don't say how readily
you dropped to your knees, the way he
turned you around so you could see
your reflection in the glass, strangely
wild that way, together with your
husband, and he so intent on repeating
the same gesture in the candlelight, as if
caught in the flicker of a silent film.

For if you dared to speak of this,
you woud be a child again, drawing
a cathedral with crayons, trying to explain
the most vivid thing you know:
the way part of you stands watch, alert
as an owl in the branches while both of you
beat blindly in the dark, unable
to remain upright, unable to hold still

as you turn and shift in the descent
like spelunkers who must find the right
passage for their very lives, the one
that has to be there somewhere, the spot
where you first entered, where the world
first flew apart, forced to break it open
with your very breath, bone, river,
blood—together and lost
as moths in a cave, flapping,
flapping toward the flame.

Dinah Berland

Old Boyfriends

I've done this before: let my hands
go hunting over the body of tonight's

lover, feeling for the bones of one lost
to me—for a familiar fit between new arms.

Something old is calling—a dark, rough
thing pressed down and away, made small

from years of not quite forgetting,
a suddenly now-glittering thing that flashes

through dark air. It's faint but undeniable—
a shadowy ticking that calls, that promises—

like a clock counting small hours only the sleepless
can hear or a heart pinned by the weight

of my head. By the sound, he's close. Close
enough to tuck my cheek into the little depression

I left in his chest. Our edges frayed now and soft,
surely we'd make a better fit...but the sound fades,

the hunt slows, and my hands come up empty.
Finished with me for the night, my new lover

rolls over, leaving me to trace contours
in the fresh sweat on his shoulder—a shining

map, a line of dashes, and there,
for this moment, this man: an X.

Anna Weaver

Letter Written on a Boarding Pass

I stole your trick, a dab of dijon whisked
into the scrambled eggs, yellow to yellow,
a little tang. I will not give you credit.
Out back, scratched in snow, a wallow
where deer have slept. You grind your teeth at night.
Let's fuck. Let's eat too much ice cream.
Let's walk the dog. You can dim the light.
Let's finally watch *Heaven's Gate*, the scene
where fresh-faced students twirl their ladies'
skirts on the lawn, the scene where lovers skate a gyre
on ice laid thick like fondant over dirt,
the scene where everything is on fire.
Make me a drink. Show me how to start
this letter: *dear friend, dear no one, dear heart.*

Juliana Gray

Survival

The female comes first to set up camp,
anchor her bed to the sliding glass door and edge
of the roof's overhang. When the sun's just

right, her handiwork glows as if spun
from solar flares. The spiders taught you:
all creation dares to disturb the universe.

The center spirals and begins to hold one, two,
three moths—wings caught in caterwaul.
This is a summer of simple breezes and simple meals.

One male approaches, all eyelash and winking
legs, tendrils of vibration along tensile lines. Then
another and another, now three, a jubilee.

There are sidelong glances, there is idling.
So many dark stars rising. Do you remember?
Sometimes there's an imperative you can't refuse.

She sucks out the eyeballs of a fly, and I
imagine her consorts find such hunger sexy.
She has patience bred into her, going

back millennia, to the time of galaxies,
incorporated. I am in charge of the moon,
porch light whose switch I flick to illumine

a map of their universe for you. Even here
an unseen hand has something to do with survival.
After coupling, she will devour one, two,

three and clothe herself in silken bandages.
And I will watch the moon rise late September over
an empty web, sheets of the bed cool with your absence.

Andrea Bates

An Equitable Distribution

The dresser gone, the highboy, and the bed,
but she had left the mirror, old, ornate,
with gilded frame and black-blotched full-length glass.
How many times had he watched her appraise
her full effect, adjusting a blouse, the drape

of a scarf, the trim of a dress, soliciting
sometimes his critique, inviting him into
small complicities—these shoes, this belt,
this scent?—while he stood behind her, doing up
a zipper he hoped later to undo?

Now all undone, the bedroom disarrayed,
unused. More convenient to sleep downstairs
because they had agreed on his and hers,
and she had picked up almost all her things.
Odd, she did not take the gilded mirror.

Well, she could come and get it when she pleased.
He looks about the room, astonished by
the mess she left: sachets, stockings, barrettes—
the stuff she didn't want. Then his reflection
disappears when he shuts the bedroom door.

Edison Jennings

Country Cream

— *Clever, Missouri 2007*

She clutches the handle, positions the base between her legs, russet-
caking across the kneecaps.
I was once like you.

Her shoulders tighten as she pushes the paddle
deeper through the thickening liquid and pulls our new friendship
out of the hazy curl of smoke that drifts from the cigarette
dangling on her cracked lips. I take the smoke in, take it as deep

inside as I can and watch the white of her knuckles
turn whiter. *Believe me,* she continues, *that road*—she pounds
the bottom of the tub, huffs—*always ends poorly.*

Thin bubbles churn to the top and burst.

     * * *

She taps the lip of the beer bottle again.

Flies disappear, quickly fade into twilight, quiet
enough to hear the wind shift a row or two as it breaks
through twenty-two acres of sweet corn fields.

We had a mountain lion, few summers back.

I say nothing, stare at the stalks, still full from the early rain,
turning to reflect the slight glow from the harvest orb.

I saw it too. Sitting right here from this porch.
Thought it was a dog at first—until it moved.
Feline.

She skims off a layer of fat.
Pours the dregs back into the wooden tub; it unravels, thick
yarn piling between us.

Word travels out here, sure as seasons.
The men tried, each morning leaving with rifles in hand,
                    but never found that trophy.

                *   *   *

I'm deep in marriage now, she confesses. We leave the cream to sour
overnight under the porch's constellation of cobwebs.

When my husband walks out to the front fields, drops to his knees,
        and prays
for enough from the crops for our family to get by on—

                    I remember why I married him.

But this life's hardest when I ask him to take me
like a teenager between the sweet stalks of our corn. Help me
remember why we wanted this farm, this family.

She rests the smooth spat across the top of the barrel and looks back
at me, to what cannot be said aloud, and the white lies that divorce

the distance between us.

It's hardest when he says nothing, refuses to come in from the
tractor.

                *   *   *

With the day's sweat dampening our undershirts and an empty bottle
half full of butts, we pretend to listen to the panting earth, and
            eventually find ourselves
hummed back into the present tense by the field's nocturnal pulse.

Still, I mutter, *I'm going to.*

Trust me, she says before she stands, drops the last smoke into
         the bottle —
that road only ends in a marriage like mine.

Our words circle with the rusted blades of the porch fan,
when I sense something stir behind the tall grass, something starved,
fierce, something that managed to slip from its own death.

Jessica Glover

Against Morning

All night the sun has waited
to bring this lace of light;
color comes to the room
without grace and too soon
we see too well to dream;
mystery was our aim—
it left no room for sleep;
now in the tangle of sheets,
we are still and touching;
we trust so much in things
we must lose in daylight;
you move and bright bands
bend on your back; the blinds
keep in what days lack.

Paul Jones

The Bride Slept In

her newly dead mother-in-law's room:
where a silver mirror
and crystal hairpin dish
still held their places
on the lace dresser scarf.
She surveyed the papered blue toile walls:
shepherds and shepherdesses,
so at ease, posed on their painted tussocks
laughing among their flutes and sheep.
Wearing her new nightgown,
white lace and satin, the bride
unpinned her hair,
placed her pins, one at a time,
in the little dish. It was quiet
in the bathroom now; so she wriggled
beneath the embroidered, yellowed, sheets.
The bathroom doorknob rattled.
The moon was bright enough
to see him, a procession of himself
coming toward her until
he stubbed his toe
on the bedside table
and roared a string of curses,
looked at her and caught himself,
and began to laugh. And she began
laughing, and he held her
laughing and under the covers
on the old sleigh bed,
a fumbling ritual—like first communion
or learning to walk in high heels.
Later they slept
in their room of almost moonlight,
sunk in the hollowed shape
of her mother-in-law, on a slope of years,
among her silver and her shepherds fading
in the dark. Out of her nightgown, out from
beneath the cocoon of sheets. His long leg
thrown over her. A long time ago.

Nora Shepard

She Spent A Season Not Looking In the Mirror

estranged from reflection,
in empty rooms, an empty bed—

a spinster by any other name—
dialing the same phone number, so that once

again, she would be able to hang up on him.

Her half sleep emergent with his own—
they'd share the under music

of their misplaced life, the two ends of the line
a kind of empty suitcase.

A braided breath; not sex exactly—

but the buttery flavor of deep night,
spilled lamplight to anoint their coupling

in a silent spring of dis-
solution.

Susan Rich

"The Girls in Their Summer Dresses," Take II

He had hurt her as he always did,
Unintentionally, these Sunday afternoons
After their morning of struggling over what to do—
They had risen late, and going back to bed
Would kill the day. Imagine him thinking that
Twenty years ago, but now he had said it
And she looked out the window, saying with her eyes,
"If we don't have each other we still have the world."

Outside on the streets, empty of cars and trucks,
The occasional cab rolled unhailed down Fifth Avenue,
For who would not walk this perfect August day,
Dry, unseasonable with a little autumn breeze
To tug at the hems of the girls in their summer dresses.
Yes, he saw them as soon as he left the apartment,
And she knew right away why it was he looked back.
"Please, don't be so obvious," she wanted to tell him,
Then hurried the pace on their walk to the park.

The future seemed dim to her now and the past
She recalled only as this morning when she sat
Idly in the big chair in her underpants and bra,
Slowly turning the pages of the *Times* to see what
He would do. Even now, sitting on the bench together,
His eyes moved away from her towards the girl,
Not even pretty, walking past them in gauzy cotton,
The sun tracing between her slender thighs,
The sun shining its otherwise painful summer light.

Stuart Dischell

Bathroom Graffiti

What is love? Girls are just
friends that give you erections.
Under promise, over deliver.

Floating between ecstasy
and despair. He told me he doesn't
miss you. We can never

just be ourselves, we can only
portray ourselves. Remember, 8

hugs a day is minimum.
Life is not an apology. Please call
for no reason.

Shannon Rayne

Waiting Up

In the sea between curled fist and ear,
I listen for your motor through the dark,

long after the dusk chorus of barking
quieted, the clink of the gate gave way

to east side sirens, and these still rooms
settled into place. Something opens

in the night, the wine buzz through my fingertips,
rasp of sheets, and though my heart beats hard

I hear them—barred owl pair in the pine
above the neighbor's house, low notes and guttural

upward thrust blanketing the roofs and the little
matching sheds. On the nightstand,

the silenced phone glows with news of you,
one hour more. I count off like thunder

their calls first near, then farther off.
Surely these are lovers reassuring one another

through the treetops, the oaks' deep shadows.
Without you here, to whom can I tell

this beauty happened? In the kitchen,
something whirs, something stirs the gate.

Laura Davenport

Escaping to Cuba

You tell me about the streets
overflowing with balconies,
and T-shirts of Ché hanging on telephone wires.
You want to sell me Cuba.
You tell me about the hotel
the color of banana peeling itself,
the paint disappearing slowly
like the extended days of the revolution.
No need to convince me.
I would sell my Honda
and buy a ticket on a single engine cargo plane;
I would sell the Buddha
I found at a garage sale.
I will follow you even if you're Castro,
even if you kiss me like a Marxist
kissing Lenin's feet,
even if you pull me away from my mother's glance.
All so that I can be
on that terrace
playing the typewriter like Hemingway,
and watching you blowing
smoke against the sunrise of Havana.
And when the fishermen below
see you dancing like Erato,
they will curse their wives and me
for having you all to myself
for one day
in that room
at sunrise.

Shahé Mankerian

Leopard

The strut says I am, ooh, much more physical than you.
I've crouched on a limb and considered giraffe.
You'd *better* climb.
I'll be up that tree on your primate ass.

Where I am men hide.
I'll slap you like the monkey you are.
Paws out, already back, slapped again from the other side.
Two three times 'til you know you've been hit.

I like the instant you cling to the claw before you flop.
You think in that moment you might get away.
I love your hope.
It makes me growl.

I'll let you get a little in before I pounce.
Oblong, imbalanced. Bet your feet slide out,
smart guy, language-man, who's serious now?
Brain, meet mister tooth.

John FitzGerald

Oconee

Only that day dawns to which we are awake.
—*Henry David Thoreau*

There are names your tongue will take to:
Tamassee Creek, Old Horse Bone Road.

A crow calls across first light,
                     and your breath eases.

You've come for the cadence of footfall,
the swish of a branch against your arm.

Past stumps & logs, mushrooms & lichens.
Huckleberry, sassafras, fern. A box turtle
                     if you're lucky.

On a stick, or on leaf mold, movement
(bright green and small):
                     a caterpillar crawls.

The memory, from another year
on another trail, of a wild turkey flushed
                     and rising from nowhere.

Tulip tree blossoms lie scattered, fallen
to pieces, each petal a tiny silk cup
                     flung down as if for you.

Sunlight laces through the canopy.
                     A pileated woodpecker
drums a tree and, winging a flash of red,
stutters away.

Soon the clean tumble of the falls.

In the air, before you and behind, always
a shadow, that slight possibility of bear.

Susan Laughter Meyers

Bird *Gnosis*

> *I will speak to you in blood language.*
> *(Answer with a tower of birds)*
> — Octavio Paz

In a drawer, the yellowed photograph labeled *before*
birth.
　　　Flesh undone, and there we are,
strata of the ridge (huge against the sky)—calcified male
/ female—

mock pinnacle and gorge.　　Hungry as lightning.

~

And wasn't it prescient　　the shadows we could
cast. Sublimely mineral　　we tried hard to bow
(be mannerly) above sea-level.

Insular geology　　　　even then.

None of that sprawling foam of lovers—
you were my taller reminiscence　　sandstone
a porous being.

~

More and more enthralled, ingrown, the nerves
wound tight.
　　　　　　　　　And one bird
(or traveling star)　　changed the terms of *strata*
for us,　the impossibly erect.

(say, *bird*　　and it sets you free like that)

~

Bells from far away suggest another life—
　　　　　　　　　　　after /over/ before.
Notes from the malleable and missing.

Can love be there, but not here?   Touch the cleft
where once my wings pushed through. Flesh never
asked for a home in space,
                              an alpha or omega.

                    ~

Sperm-swaddled egg
(yours, mine). Anxious in time.   Infant
sprung from the groans of others.
                              What part
of us was made to face the wind—
heart medium
bird breath
midwife palms
set for emergence?   (balled-up   sacked
then   stretched to screaming)

                    ~

And don't forget that old tantrika dizzying the universe
back to a single cell.
                    What split us in two, from down
to deeper down?
Legs jointed, double breasted, and finally sexed.

                    ~

But before our brief confinement we were birds

fresh from the sea   (hollow bones in a body flying)

screech above
                and the great feathered spiral turning

Cry for me and suck the salt wind in

                    —after Picasso's "L'Histoire Geologique"

Katherine Soniat

Luna Half

a wing lies on the path
its foot fringed with fine white feathers

its luff and leech dark red and
growing from the luff like a flower
off its stem a single eye the wing
is coated in a pale green dust

my fingers disarray no matter
how carefully i try to hold it

later i pass a mating pair
hanging like a single vulva

from a leaf everything
even the moon so frail

Lola Haskins

Father's Day, 2014

We play soccer, picnic, grill chicken under foil-wrapped bricks. My daughter so enamored with her daddy that she pores over the trophy catalog, picks out a ribbon for him in yellow, her favorite color. It says "Fourth Place." She is so pleased. She pays with her own money. "Fourth place," I tease my husband. "That's better than I thought you'd do." Somehow, I do not think of my father until the kids are in bed and I'm washing dishes. Somehow, I'd spent the day not worrying that people always say abusers must be forgiven. Forgiveness the bitter only parts of the tongue can taste. Forgiveness the hot coal swallowed and swallowed again. My hands and arms so hidden by soapy water that someone looking would swear that parts of me were missing.

Karen Skolfield

Dressing the Wound

He knew I had the heart to hurt him—
me, still a teen, with years of practice
in defiance, words slicing like a scalpel.
Do it fast!, he said, and holding my breath,

I put one hand on his chest and with the other yanked
the medical tape, ripping the hair from his skin,
the wide strip denuded and blushing. My slow fingers
unwrapped the surgical site, and I pulled away

pus-filled gauze to re-dress the incision, a slit half-open
like eyelids closing over a pupil, the hard, clear tube
dug into his side. Cloudy, pleural fluid oozed through it.
My dad smilingly called me his nurse:

Let me pay you.
                    My body jerked tight,
but I kept on, patting down new tape, palm-to-pectoral,
a blind girl reading his heart.

Elizabeth W. Jackson

Abandoned House, Saigon

Two swallows fly in a broken window, sweeping under
yellow orchids tumbling from the rotted frame.

The ghost up there has stopped her complaining
while out in the rain below a tarp, a girl selling soup

squats by the curb slicing tiny hoops of chili,
piling little heaps of red on a white dish.

Did the ghost upstairs learn English or French?
Where did she intend to go? Why does she linger?

How her lips must burn when her fingers brush them.
One swallow darts out the darkened window

while over in L.A., stuck in traffic, some Vietnamese guy
remembers this street, the vendor, the house lying almost empty.

John Balaban

To Be of Use

This is all I want. This is all I need.
To stand in the yard with that committed maple
As he moans overhead, shedding leaf and seed.
To offer my chin, my ear, my breast and lapel.
To stand still, still enough for this wren.
To have her make of my mouth a nest,
Be her perch in evening, and morning then
Feel her small, determined head thrust
And push and part my lips.
To watch the world take her away
Into the deafening white, feel wingtip's
Touch upon on my cheek, and say
For once, What more than this? What wish?
The sun of my mouth, her feathers lit.

Lee Colin Thomas

Melt

We awoke to two owls calling,
their brief questions skipping along the snowpack
as they tried to find each other.
One was close, almost right over us.
We were soothed by the sound of their loneliness.

When the horizon blushed, they grew quiet
(having arrived at last together, or resigned to be apart),
and we saw the morning would be clear and fine
though wrapped all around with white.

Later, the ponies moved off from the barn,
laying out the shapes of themselves
as lumbering as mammoths
in the snow that balled in their feet and slipped them.

There was an indentation in front of the gate
and another behind it where a mule deer
had leapt over on its way through.

In the afternoon, the ground glinted as it threw sunlight back,
warming bases of scant clouds with its albedo,
and snow slowly began to give way to water.
The roof rumbled, sloughing off the first part of its winter weight.

Things we recognized would soon start to be uncovered.
Icicles formed and dropped from the eaves.

The fence rails crossed in shadows
blue and stark with a hardened intent on the shrinking white,
as if to write some prophecy we'd decipher if the lines
could better arrange themselves.

Chera Hammons

Devotion

In my twenties I exhaled into the safe testimony
of a man, let him pull on the hand
that had been broken many times. He put it
on his mouth and near his blue eyes. I didn't know
the long rope of touch could save me—sinew woman,
woman of bowers and sagebrush, cramp-bark
and shepherds, woman untold. He couldn't understand
the fissures and clefts of my tribe,

but he memorized the prayers I sang
because he saw how they opened my marrow.
Nine months we entered the temple and sat
to study oppression. I had learned it before. Each week
at our lessons, we niggled despair: the pogroms
and the curses, the sweet pulp of ancient interpretation.

When we left that office (a mountain of oral decree
and denomination), the city was larger—all din
and feasts as others worshipped action and shopping
and ordinary need. In the sanctuary on Saturdays,
my blue-eyed man tapped on my shoulder to say God
stepped into every line of the book. Was that important?

I knew the prayers as glass hills and gold islands.
Not rules. Not commandments. I had always been looking
for something less certain. Prayers held center; the chant
was a curtain drawn from the ark. A magic
of melody carried the meaning. Perhaps our outer walls
were not isolation. No, he wouldn't have memory,
but he could forecast murmur and praise. Could see
what he saw, even pull closer, perceive all the gleam.

Lauren Camp

How We Were Caught

That first time you didn't warn me
you decided to claim a souvenir:

I only learned about the fork after
I pulled you close and felt tines

prick my hip. I wanted to show you
I too could love dangerously.

Our pockets soon rattled
whenever we left the scene.

Strewn across my Buick's backseat,
spoons from Sweet Grass Wok clanged

against crackers from the Crab Shack.
We lasted almost four months—

before we were pinched fleeing Embers,
steak knives in waistbands

gouging our hips. Afterwards,
once we had paid our fines

and completed community service,
we couldn't go anywhere.

Even places we'd never hit
kept our picture by the register.

Soon we fell apart. Still,
I sometimes think of you

during summer storms
when metal moves against metal—

right before the sky cracks open
and the heat washes away.

Noel Sloboda

Traveler's Lament

> *Should we have stayed home and dreamed of here? Where*
> *should we be today?*
> — Elizabeth Bishop, "Questions of Travel"

I miss the man who sells us wine, suggests
the Covey Run,

Rainbow Grocery's neon orange tennis ball
tangerine stacks.

I miss the flower shop with its bundles of African Daisies,
Queen Anne's Lace.

I miss our street, gossamer blossoms stuck like unlucky insects
to windshields, headlights.

I even miss the neighbor's pick-up truck turning over, at six am,
twenty Hoovers and a leaf blower,

clang of dumpster lid. Futility of sweeping sunflower hulls
from the walk,

the mailman bringing (politely, daily) more and more
of nothing.

I miss lugging the trash to the curb in a robe
about to slip open,

the hot water tank we easily emptied
each time we made love in the tub.

Martha Silano

For Telly the Fish

Telly's favorite artist was Alice Neel.
When he first came to my house,
I propped up her bright yellow shade with open
window & a vase of flowers (post card size)
behind his first fish bowl. I thought
it might give him something
to look at, like the center
of a house you keep coming
back to, a hearth, a root
for your eye. It was a
wondering in me that came up with that
thought, a kind of empathy
across my air & through his
water, maybe the first
word that I propped up between us
in case he could
hear. Telly would stare at the painting
for hours, hanging there with his glassy
eyes wide
open. At night he'd glide to the
bottom, as if it were a warm
bed, & lie there
sort of dreaming, his eyes
gray & dim &
thoughtless. For months he came back
to her, the way a critic or lover
can build a whole
lifetime on the study of one
great work. I don't know why
he stopped, maybe it was when
he first noticed
me, the face above my hand
feeding for, sometimes, when I'd set the food
on top, he'd still watch me, eye
to eye, as if saying, food
isn't enough. Once, when I

bent, he jumped up out of the water & kissed
my lips. What is a fish's kiss like?
You'd think it would be
cold, slimy, but it was
quick, nippy, hard. Maybe it was just
what I expected. For all
our fears of
touch, it takes so long
to learn how to take in.

I guess I did all the wrong
things—the fish
medicine that smelled, measured
carefully for his ounce of weight,
for his gills worked
so slow, & he lay still,
tipped over slightly,
like a dead boat.
How do you stop the hurt
of having to breathe?

After, I took him to the middle of the
yellow bridge right near the
Andy Warhol museum—I had put a paper towel
in a painted egg and laid him in it. &, at the top,
I opened the casket & emptied him out
into the water.

Toi Derricotte

God's Harem

Last night the stars
made a spectacle of themselves
hanging naked at heaven's
doorway, calling *here, here*.

I lay beneath their fiery fingers,
breathing. My body came and came
until it could yield no more.
Again, I could hear the lapping
of the lake, the night wind rowing.

Later in the kitchen I poured
a glass of water. Starlight
so framed the cedars beyond
I drank in the dark.

Late morning, a rowboat culls
lily pads by old pilings, one
sprouting a huckleberry bush.
A man and two children drift
in the possibilities.

I want to tell them the hour
is wrong: rise early, work by lantern.
But this is the time they have.
This is the time we all have, doing
what can be done.

Just now the man
bends over a pole, raising the arc,
four hands in the grip. He teaches
a wider cast, easy as gnats,
there, wait for the tug.

The other child dangles her hand
off the low stern. The disturbance
plays itself out in the wake
of mallards, white-collared emissaries.

What happens here will be remembered.
The coolness of lake water in one's hand,
the green, beckoning, the song
of the line traveling the air.

All this the stars notice. They wait
like bass, bluegill, rainbow trout.
When the veil of sun drops, they will begin
their radiant display, casting
luminous dust, their eternal desire.

Carol Barrett

Guinea Pig

When the small hill
of the mother's body stayed still,
I knew she'd died.
Fanny sat in the woodchips beside her.

When I returned with a ziplock bag,
she lay right on top of her, making
a soft, almost inaudible sound—
her mourning strangely the same

as any other I've known—
the same perfect limpness
of one body thrown over another
like a hopeless cloth,

and the sound of deepest sorrow,
muffled as though it came
from the center of a gigantic stone.

I couldn't bring myself to move her.
All afternoon she lay
on the sudden silence of
her mother's heart

and on the slower news
of the body, which still
offered a fading warmth.

Sally Bliumus-Dunn

This Is My Plan

In the normal course of things, you'll die
before I die, older than I
and male, and therefore burning up your life
faster than my woman's body can
no matter how I'd wish
this body could vanish without you to hold it here.
Chances are we won't go down in flames
from skies between the place we live
and anywhere we go to look at paintings
showing other pairs—John and Salomé,
Danae and her lap of coins,
Apollo and Daphne, Adam and God, Adam and Eve,
Eve and the snake, old and affectionate Dutch couples.
And chances are we won't fall off some bridge
together, having done our falling years ago.

These are the things I'll never do again:
I won't eat lobster, sing the hymn called Hyferdol,
see the ballet company we saw on our first date,
ride a German train, choose a man's tie, drink English Breakfast tea.
I will not trim the beard and hair of any other man.
I'll burn the clothes of mine you liked, and
all the cards we played Gin Rummy with.
I swear, I will not harm myself, will not
fill my eyes with ashes, or steal dirt from your grave
to stop my ears, will not cut my skin
to let the howling out. I will not die.

Devon Miller-Duggan

Prince Albert's Hand

Queen Victoria slept with dead Albert's nightshirt,
ordered his shaving kit set out each day. But why

a plaster cast of his hand? Refusing to put on the robes
of state, wearing mourning for forty years, I see

the heroic logic. But if I woke in an empty bed, breathed
your scent from your soft shirt and gripped your

plaster hand, it would point toward my tired breasts,
mock the bulk of my body. Empires rise and fall, reckless,

faithless. Clerks wash their faces and clean their teeth.
Victoria gets up from bed, touches the hand, kisses

its fingers and leaves it all day to gather motes of dust.
I kiss you, dear one, the scent of lemons on your hands.

Barbara Daniels

Memorial Video

When I see you now, not so changed from who you were,
I am reminded of how snow fell at the window
with the church steeple and the mustard-colored Victorian,
our neighborhood Women's Club, a stately dinosaur
even then. And sadness? What could we know of it?
Night lit blue, the first time at love, it was impossible
to mistake what it made in us, a sort of slick patience
and the sharp odor of snow. And all along you were
leaving first, your things, drawings and a bird,
your farewell the unthinkable way you come back.

Jeffrey Greene

A Visit to my Aunt's Garden
While She's in the Hospital Slowly Dying

The sun whitens by design,
poised among the midday hours,
the air at the end
of a long, spent sigh.
It's quiet here
where tomatoes huddle
on soft-haired vines,
yellowed leaves clutching
an old vibrancy.

Coneflowers grow reckless
blotting noxious weeds,
as birds flash
blue, coursing the literature
of their stories.
There are no prints, even faint,
of her shoes,
the rain-pocked dirt dry
where swollen-bellied squash lay
gnawed, a bee buried
in a lone, late blossom.

Marylin Hervieux

Elegy

Early on in the city
on weekends claimed by fog
I came back to your farmstead,
your emptied creek-side
shanty house
from my laboratory wage work
with pockets full of micropipettes
and stolen white gloves
as if to outfit a regiment of ghost butlers
in an imagined antebellum manor
neither of us, if offered, would inhabit—
but I still saw the manor's cut crystal
glinting in night-frost on the fescue
beneath persimmon trees
where great horned owls left
bones to bleach. These nights
lately—with the fine rain singing
through ragweed, through mulberry
we'd kept for feeding ducks, the silkworm farm
we planned to someday have—I swim
the wild wheat that shines
like a lake to far back acres. I unstring
my jewelry, tarnishing from its work week—
in the city of sooted brick and grimy
air—from my neck
and wrists, spread the legs
of the wooden-runged ladder, and hang
it in arcs inside the fig bower's
hay rick ribcage,
displayed like ceremonial
specimens pinned to felt-lined glass cases
by the fig's knobby twigs. Deprived of ceremony
I find nothing
in my hands but unmoored
symbols: one week I caught june bugs
in a jar every night to feed the ducks,

or once burnt old letters
from lovers and the First National Bank alike,
so methodically, as if a prayer
summoning spirits
to the occasion could ever come
from cynics' lips. Look down
through the layers of history cat's-cradling
between us: unwillingly—
as algae on creek stones
loosed downstream rejoins indistinct matter—
we forget.

Miriam Bird Greenberg

The Lovers at Eighty

Fluted light from the window finds her
sleepless in the double bed, her eyes

measuring the chevron angle his knees make
under the coverlet. She is trying to recall

the last time they made love. It must have been
in shadows like these, the morning his hands

took their final tour along her shoulders and down
over the pearls of her vertebrae

to the cool dunes of her hips, his fingers
executing solemn little figures

of farewell. Strange—it's not so much
the long engagement as the disengagement

of their bodies that fills the hollow
curve of memory behind her eyes—

how the moist, lovestrung delicacy
with which they let each other go

had made a sound like taffeta
while decades flowed across them like a veil.

Marilyn L. Taylor

Transfiguration

What we think we were—
an apple, lovers, democracy—
becomes something else,

digesting peel
and core, tyranny
or anarchy,

a tree being
chopped down
for a mall,

my face turns old,
yours remains
somehow

as I pictured it
sitting by the fire
at last light

reading what
becomes mind and soul
wrapped in a cloak—

a new day,
another meal,
someone else's life.

David Radavitch

Cutting His Hair a Year Later

A year after chemotherapy,
his hair is baby fuzz dark
as the shadows that lean
over my shoulder. Here
in the bathroom light
with the electric hum
of clippers, I hesitate.
For a year he's been bald
as a newborn.
For a year his scalp wore
a clean shine I never knew.

In a crowd
I couldn't pick him out
until I remembered which
hat he wore. I'd like to think
the awful year is past,
but in this harsh light
truth stands stacked in bottles
and jars.

Carefully
I glide the scissoring
blades around his ears,
slowly across the back
of his neck...that tender, so
vulnerable spot. I even out
this soft growth, this hard-earned,
hard-won fuzz remembering
how needles and tubes bruised
his thinned arms, made them
magenta, blue, deep purple before
they finally faded to yellow and tan.

Now his hair is blacker
than before, thicker
than before and I cry
cutting it. So glad, so glad
to have the job to do.

Ruth Moose

Unmarked Grave

All I want is a single hand,
A wounded hand if that is possible.
        —Federico Garcia Lorca

Beautiful man, with your brows of broken ashes
and eyes that migrate in winter,

a hollow in your hand
where the moon fell through.

I could have kissed your mouth,
passed an olive with my tongue,
the aftertaste of canaries on our breath.

But the shriek of the little hour
is spent, and there is no road back.

The day it happened
there were no good boys
or dovecots filled with virgins,

just a sun imploding
like a sack of rotten oranges,

the scent of basil
from the grove near your home
and the piano that still waits for you.

No one will remember
the coward who shot you,
but the sheets,

the white sheets you sail on,
coming home.

Lois P. Jones

Dear Everything,

I lost the words I had written
on the occasion of your birth—

something about hands
overlaid and locking, hands climbing

an imaginary trellis of our years.
Those words fell to the stone-eared

ground as the petals of your flowering
almond shrub do late each spring.

But today that tree is at its peak,
ringed by a gathering of wrens and grackles.

How you'd love the fresh look
of these blooms, the raucous

celebration on the lawn.

Cal Freeman

Prana

"Everyone needs a good requiem mass
now and then," you said, Patrick,

while we sat in El Cedro de Libano
in Merida, drinking red wine.

Raised Catholic, you no longer
believed, but the music the mass

had inspired? You'd grant Mozart
and Berlioz deity, not to mention

the Latin that pulses through
medieval chants. I'm sure you kept

faith in that, too, not to mention tequila
and jokes about Mexican dogs,

those pitiable creatures about which
the radio sang, "Perro, Perro, Perro,

que noble animal!" We laughed
over our Frijol con Puerco

at that one. And at my tipsy gaffe
before postres arrived, wanting "Cafe

con chico." The waiter laughed,
too. Back home, we'd often stand talking

in parking lots or vegetable stalls
in the supermarket. You knew

the best wines, the best cognac,
how to find the best flat in Firenze.

Being no Buddhist, I don't chide
my monkey mind, leaping from memory

to memory, refusing to let you no longer be
here. My door's always open. Threshold

a scatter of marigold petals. Bottle
of Sangiovese. Uncorked. Breathing.

Kathryn Stripling Byer

Lightning

No wind, no rain, but every bolt that staggered
from the cumulus that night seemed to raise
a frenzy in the hemispheres of his brain.

I held my husband's head in the damp nest
of my palms, watched the tremors in his eyes
turn and turn like tiny whirlwinds, until

all that I loved was lost in lightning, darkness,
fire. And when the anaesthetic began
to ferry him down a calmer circle,

to wait out the night, I praised his strength,
the goodness of his body—every working cell
and keeper of his passage I prayed defend him,

I let him go. Near midnight the nurse shone
her torch over the still lakes of his eyes,
and I thought of sleeping Odysseus safe beneath

his quilt of leaves, his face smooth like wax-paper,
no piercing rain, no drenched gales or beating heat
upon him. No movement, she said. No light.

Leanne O'Sullivan

Vulpine

> *Yet here was the thing in the midst of the bones,*
> *the wide-eyed innocent fox inviting me to play...*
> *The universe was swinging around in some fantastic*
> *fashion to present its face, and the face was so small*
> *the universe itself was laughing.*
> — Loren Eisley, *The Unexpected Universe*

My love, I would set you again on that trail you loved
to run, your hair still long from another era,
your heart the beat, your mind all music—
Getz, Parker, Bach, Gillespie,
Debussy, Stravinsky, Coltrane—your own
improvisations running alongside
racing, shaping what your fingers
would play into the wind.

I remember April I remember you

                         I remember
how you lay curled in pain, your spine
collapsing like a column of smoke,
                    your hands
knotted with arthritis that took your flute
out of your grasp, but not the spirit of it, and not
the love you had for me, which depth
I've realized late, able to see it only in the daily dark
that is your whole absence—disappearance so immense
there's no measure, no metaphor for it—
how the meaning of life is life, and the meaning
of death is life, no delusion of heaven intervening
in that tight-woven tapestry, no uplifting
wing.
               Only the fox came
came on the night you died, strange
angel the color of gold fire,
                   trickster lifted
whole from a child's picture book,

lifting his delicate feet in the winespill
of moonlight that held the whole backyard
hostage to clarity. The planets
were in a rare, perfect alignment
altering *this one night* with light uncanny
as the fox that danced straight toward me.
With eyes full of moon, it danced almost
close enough for me to touch, danced
as if to music, as if it would speak
in that language some single thing
not available elsewhere.
                       Beauty perhaps,
which may be holy and once only
and all we have.

Betty Adcock

Author Biographies

Betty Adcock is the author of seven poetry collections, six from LSU Press, notably *Intervale: New and Selected Poems* and *Slantwise*. Her most recent collection is *Widow Poems* (Jacar Press). She has held Fellowships from the National Endowment for the Arts, the North Carolina Arts Council, and the Guggenheim Foundation. Her work appears in many journals and two Pushcart Prize anthologies. She has taught as Kenan Writer-in-Residence at Meredith College, in NCSU's Graduate Writing Program, and for ten years was a faculty member of the low residency Warren Wilson MFA Program for Writers.

Kelli Russell Agodon is a poet, writer, and editor from the Northwest. Her recent books are *Hourglass Museum* and *The Daily Poet: Day-By-Day Prompts for Your Writing Practice*. She's the cofounder of Two Sylvias Press & codirector of Poets on the Coast.

John Balaban is the author of twelve books of poetry and prose, which have won The Academy of American Poets' Lamont Prize, a National Poetry Series Selection, and two nominations for the National Book Award. His *Locusts at the Edge of Summer: New and Selected Poems* won the William Carlos Williams Award from the Poetry Society of America. He teaches at NC State University in Raleigh. His poem "Abandoned House, Saigon" was previously published in *Granta*.

Carol Barrett holds doctorates in both clinical psychology and creative writing. She teaches for Union Institute & University. The recipient of an NEA Fellowship in Poetry, she has published two collections, including the prize-winning *Calling in the Bones* (Ashland Poetry Press), and over 200 poems in magazines and anthologies.

Andrea Bates is the author of the chapbooks *Origami Heart* (Toadlily Press) and *The Graveyard Sonnets* (Finishing Line Press). Her work has appeared in a variety of literary journals in the U.S. and abroad. Originally from Connecticut, she has called Wilmington, NC, home since 2001.

Roberta Beary is the haibun editor of *Modern Haiku*; she tweets her photoku @shortpoemz. Her haiku narrative *The Unworn Necklace* was named a William Carlos Williams PSA finalist. Her recent book *Deflection* features her haibun and haiku. She travels worldwide to speak on the art of the short poem.

Dinah Berland's poems have appeared in *The Antioch Review, The Iowa Review, One, Ploughshares*, and many other publications. She received her MFA in poetry at Warren Wilson College and an international prize from *The Atlanta Review*. She is the editor of *Hours of Devotion: Fanny Neuda's Book of Prayers for Jewish Women*. "Your Secret Life" was first published, in an earlier version, in *Yellow Silk*.

Sally Bliumis-Dunn teaches modern poetry at Manhattanville College. She recieved her MFA in Poetry from Sarah Lawrence in 2002. Her poems have appeared in *The Paris Review, Prairie Schooner, The Bellevue Literary Review,* the *NYT*, on the PBS News Hour, *The Writer's Almanac* and The Academy of American Poets' Poem-a-Day site. In 2002, she was a finalist for the *Nimrod*/Hardman Pablo Neruda Prize. Her two books, *Talking Underwater* and *Second Skin,* were published by Wind Publications.

Chana Bloch's *Swimming in the Rain: New & Selected Poems, 1980-2015* includes work from *The Secrets of the Tribe, The Past Keeps Changing, Mrs. Dumpty*, and *Blood Honey*. Bloch co-translated The Song of Songs and Israeli poets Yehuda Amichai and Dahlia Ravikovitch. "The Joins" will appear in *The Best American Poetry 2015* and *Pushcart Prize XL*.

Kierstin Bridger is a Colorado writer and winner of The Mark Fischer Prize and the 2015 ACC Writer's Studio Award. Her work has appeared or is forthcoming in *Fugue,* The Lascaux Prize 2015 Anthology, *Memoir, Thrush Poetry Journal, Mason's Road,* and others. She earned her MFA degree at Pacific University.

Kathryn Stripling Byer lives in the highlands of western North Carolina. Her work has received the Laughlin Award for a second book from the Academy of American Poets, the Hanes Poetry Award from The Fellowship of Southern Writers, and Book of the Year awards from the NC Literary and Historical Association and the Southern Independent Booksellers Alliance. She served for five years as the state's first woman Poet Laureate.

Poet and radio host **Lauren Camp** is the author of two books, most recently *The Dailiness*, winner of the National Federation of Press Women Poetry Prize. Her third book, *One Hundred Hungers*, won the Dorset Prize (Tupelo Press, 2016). "Devotion" was first published in *About Place Journal*.

Hélène Cardona is the author of *Dreaming My Animal Selves* (Salmon Poetry), *Life in Suspension* (Salmon Poetry, 2016), *The Astonished Universe* (Red Hen Press), and the translations *Ce que portons* (Editions du Cygne, 2014), and *Beyond Elsewhere* (White Pine Press, 2016). She co-edits *Dublin Poetry Review* and *Fulcrum: An Anthology of Poetry and Aesthetics*. "My Mother Ceridwen" is from *Life in Suspension* (Salmon Poctry, 2016) First published in *The Original Van Gogh's Ear Anthology*.

Maxine Chernoff is the author of 14 books of poems, most recently *Here* (Counterpath Press). She chairs the Creative Writing Department at SFSU and recently read her poems in Exeter, Plymouth, Bath and London, as well as in Salerno, Italy.

Dr. Johnson Cheu is an Assistant Professor in the Dept. of Writing, Rhetoric and American Cultures at Michigan State University. He has published scholarly articles in Disability Studies and Popular Culture Studies. His poetry and creative essays have also appeared widely. He serves on the editorial board for the *Journal of Literary and Cultural Disability Studies*.

Joshua Coben's first book, *Maker of Shadows* (Texas Review Press 2010), won the X.J. Kennedy Poetry Prize. His poems have appeared in *Atlanta Review*, *The Evansville Review*, *Pleiades*, *Poet Lore*, and other journals. Born and raised in St. Louis, he spent two years in France before moving to the Boston area, where he teaches elementary school.

Barbara Conrad is the author of *Wild Plums* (Future Cycle) and *The Gravity of Color* (Main Street Rag) and editor of *Waiting for Soup: An Anthology of Art and Poetry from Urban Ministry Center.* Barbara's work has appeared in *Tar River Poetry, Sow's Ear*, and *Charlotte Viewpoint* and in the anthologies *...and love..., Icarus* and *Kakalak*. She plays West African drums with Charlotte Community Drummers.

Howard L. Craft is a poet and an award-winning playwright. He is the author of a book of poems, *Across The Blue Chasm*. His poetry also appears in *Home is Where: An Anthology of African-American Poets from the Carolinas*, edited by Kwame Dawes.

Barbara Daniels's *Rose Fever: Poems* was published by WordTech Press and her chapbooks *Moon Kitchen*, *Black Sails* and *Quinn & Marie* by Casa de Cinco Hermanas Press. She received three Individual Artist Fellowships from the New Jersey State Council on the Arts, most recently in 2014.

Laura Davenport's poems have appeared in *One, Crab Orchard Review, Meridian, New South, Best New Poets 2009* and *Boxcar Poetry Review*. She is the recipient of a Meridian Editors' Prize, a Hackney Literary award, and the *Richmond Magazine/* James River Writers Best Poem award.

Susan de Sola, an American poet living in the Netherlands, has published poems in *The Hudson Review, American Arts Quarterly*, and *The Hopkins Review*, among many other venues. A translator and a recipient of the David Reid Poetry Translation Prize, she holds a PhD from The Johns Hopkins University. This poem originally appeared in *The Raintown Review*.

Toi Derricotte is the author of *The Undertaker's Daughter* (University of Pittsburgh Press, 2011) and four earlier collections of poetry, including *Tender*, winner of the 1998 Paterson Poetry Prize. Her literary memoir, *The Black Notebooks* received the 1998 Anisfield-Wolf Book Award for Non-Fiction and was a *New York Times* Notable Book of the Year. Her many honors include the 2012 Paterson Poetry Prize for Sustained Literary Achievement, the 2012 PEN/Voelcker Award for Poetry, the Lucille Medwick Memorial Award from the Poetry Society of America, two Pushcart Prizes and the Distinguished Pioneering of the Arts Award from the United Black Artists. Derricotte is the co-founder of Cave Canem Foundation (with Cornelius Eady), Professor Emerita at the University of Pittsburgh and a Chancellor of the Academy of American Poets.

Stuart Dischell is the author of *Good Hope Road,* a National Poetry Series Selection, *Evenings & Avenues, Dig Safe,* and *Backwards Days*—all from Penguin Poets—and the chapbooks *Animate Earth* and *Touch Monkey*. He teaches in the MFA Program in Creative Writing at the University of North Carolina Greensboro.

Susan Elbe is the author of *The Map of What Happened*, winner of the 2012 Backwaters Press Prize and the 2013 Julie Suk Award from Jacar Press, as well as *Eden in the Rearview Mirror* (Word Poetry), *Where Good Swimmers Drown* (Concrete Wolf Press) and *Light Made from Nothing* (Parallel Press). "Horses in Virginia in November" first appeared in *Where Good Swimmers Drown*, winner of the Concrete Wolf Press 2011 Chapbook prize.

John FitzGerald is an award-winning poet, editor and attorney for the disabled. He is the author of six books, the most recent of which are Favorite Bedtime Stories and The Mind. He's been widely published in journals and anthologies, notably World Literature Today, which first published "Leopard." He was editor of the Law Review.

Cal Freeman was born and raised in Detroit. His poems have appeared in many journals including *The Cortland Review, The Drunken Boat, Ninth Letter, The Journal,* and *Birmingham Poetry Review.* He has been nominated for Pushcart Prizes in both poetry and creative nonfiction. His first collection of poems, *Brother of Leaving,* was recently published by Antonin Artaud Publications.

Ana Garza G'z has an MFA from California State University, Fresno. Fifty-seven of her poems have appeared in various journals and anthologies, with one forthcoming in *Kaleidoscope*. She works as a lecturer, translator, and interpreter.

Jessica Glover teaches for the English department and the Gender and Women's Studies program at Oklahoma State University. She has an MA in English from Missouri State. Her work appears in *American Literary Review, Aesthetica, Magma Poetry, Reed Magazine, So to Speak*, and MuseWrite's *Shifts: An Anthology of Women's Growth through Change,* among others. She won the 2013 Rash Awards and the 2013 Edwin Markham Prize for Poetry.

Juliana Gray is the author of *Roleplay* and *Anne Boleyn's Sleeve*, winner of the 2013 Winged City Chapbook Press poetry contest. An Alabama native, she lives in western New York and teaches at Alfred University. "Letter Written on a Boarding Pass" previously appeared in *The Journal*.

Jaki Shelton Green is a poet, creativity coach, teacher, cultural activist. Her books include *Feeding the Light*(Jacar Press*), Dead on Arrival, Dead on Arrival and New Poems, Conjure Blues, singing a tree into dance, breath of the song* (all Carolina Wren Press). The recipient of many awards, she was recently inducted into the North Carolina Literary Hall of Fame. She lives in Mebane, North Carolina.

Jeffrey Greene is the author of four collections of poetry, a cross-genre book, a memoir, and three personalized nature books; the latest, *Wild Edibles,* is forthcoming in 2016. He is a professor at the American University of Paris and teaches for the Pan-European Low Residency MFA program.

Lucinda Grey co-edited *Southern Poetry Review* for several years. She is the author of five books of poetry: *The Blue Hills: After the Life of Maud Gonne,* winner of the *Comstock Review* Jessie Bryce Niles Award, *The Woman Who Has Eaten the Moon* (Wind Press), *Ribbon Around a Bomb,* which won the Quentin R. Howard Poetry Prize, *Martin Flores and the House of Dreams,* and *Letter to No Address.*

Miriam Bird Greenberg is the author of two collections: *All night in the new country* and *Pact-Blood, Fever Grass.* She is a recipient of a Stegner Fellowship, and fellowships from the NEA, the Poetry Foundation, and the Provincetown Fine Arts Work Center. "Elegy" has appeared in *The Queer South* anthology and *Verse Daily*.

Chera Hammons lives in Amarillo, Texas. Her work has most recently appeared in *Beloit Poetry Journal, Raleigh Review, Rattle, Sugar House Review, Tar River Poetry, Tupelo Quarterly*, and *Valparaiso Poetry Review*. Her chapbook *Amaranthine Hour* received the 2012 Jacar Press Chapbook Award. She serves on the editorial board of *One*.

Lola Haskins's work has appeared in *The Atlantic, London Review of Books, Georgia Review, Prairie Schooner*, and elsewhere. *How Small, Confronting Morning*, forthcoming from Jacar Press, will be her fourteenth poetry collection. Previous efforts include *Hunger*, which won the 1992 Iowa Poetry Prize, *Desire Lines, New and Selected Poems* (BOA), *Extranjera* (Story Line), *Forty-Four Ambitions for the Piano* (University Press of Florida). *The Grace to Leave* (Anhinga) and *Still, the Mountain (*Paper Kite*)* both won Florida Book Awards.

Marylin Hervieux's poetry appears in *Kakalak, Kalliope, North Carolina Literary Review, Tar River Poetry,* and the NC Arts Council's Poets-of-the-Week Series. She received a Literary Artist Project Grant from the Orange County (NC) Arts Council enabling her to teach poetry workshops to special needs groups in the community.

Chloe Honum is the author of *The Tulip-Flame,* which was selected by Tracy K. Smith as winner of the 2013 Cleveland State University Poetry Center First Book Prize. She is the recipient of a Ruth Lilly Fellowship from the Poetry Foundation and a Pushcart Prize.

Elizabeth W. Jackson is a practicing psychologist and writer of published essays and poems. Mainly, she loves poetry though, and her recent work has appeared or is forthcoming in *Zone 3, Measure,* and *The Southern Poetry Anthology Volume VII: North Carolina.* In 2014, she won the James Applewhite Poetry Prize. "Dressing the Wound" first appeared in *The McNeese Review.*

Author of twenty books of translation, criticism, and anthologies, **Richard Jackson** has won Fulbright, Guggenheim, NEA, and NEH fellowships, had five Pushcart appearances, and received the Medal of Freedom from the President of Slovenia for Literary and Humanitarian work in the Balkans. His most recent poetry books are *Retrievals, Out of Place,* and *Resonance.*

Edison Jennings's poems have appeared in several journals and anthologies. Jacar Press published his chapbook, *Reckoning,* in 2013. *Blue Fifth Review* will publish one of his poems in 2016. He lives in Abingdon, Virginia and is currently working on a second chapbook.

Lois P. Jones is Poetry Editor of *Kyoto Journal.* Some publications include *Tupelo Quarterly, Narrative Magazine, The Warwick Review, One,* and *Cider Press Review.* Lois won the 2012 *Tiferet* Prize and the 2012 *Liakoura Prize* and her work was long-listed in the 2014 National Poetry Competition (UK) out of 13,000 entries. Her poem "Unmarked Grave" was previously published in *American Poetry Journal.*

Paul Jones published a chapbook, *What the Welsh and Chinese Have In Common*, in which "Against Morning" appeared. Recent publications include poems in anthologies about travel, food, love and in a special tabloid on Trash as well as a longish poem in *Best American Erotic Poems: 1800-Present* (Scribners).

Debra Kaufman's *Delicate Thefts* was published this year by Jacar Press. She is the author of *The Next Moment* (Jacar 2010) and *A Certain Light* (Emrys 1996) as well as three chapbooks and many plays. Her poems have appeared in many anthologies and magazines, including *Spillway, Virginia Quarterly, The Greensboro Review*, and *North Carolina Literary Review*. "How Dreamy They Are, and Beautiful" was first published in *Poetry East*. She is an editor for *One*.

Tina Kelley's second collection of poetry, *Precise*, was published in 2013 by Word Press, publisher of her first collection, *The Gospel of Galore*, winner of a 2003 Washington State Book Award. She co-authored *Almost Home: Helping Kids Move from Homelessness to Hope*, (2012) a national bestseller about homeless young people, and lives in New Jersey.

Sally Rosen Kindred is the author of two books from Mayapple Press, *No Eden* and *Book of Asters*, and a chapbook, *Darling Hands, Darling Tongue,* from Hyacinth Girl Press. Her poems have appeared in *Quarterly West, The Journal, Linebreak, Verse Daily*, and elsewhere.

Alan King is the author of DRIFT. He's a Cave Canem graduate fellow and holds an MFA from the University of Southern Maine's Stonecoast Program. His poems have been featured on NPR, local public radio and in several publications. He's a two-time Best of the Net and Pushcart Prize nominee.

Richard Krawiec's third poetry collection, *Women Who Loved Me Despite* (Press53) was published in 2015. He has won fellowships from the National Endowment for the Arts, and the North Carolina Arts Council (twice). In addition to poetry, he has published two novels, a story collection, four plays, and numerous pieces of nonfiction. His work appears in *Shenandoah, sou'wester, Chataqua Literary Review, Dublin Review,* and elsewhere. He is founder of Jacar Press, and teaches online at UNC Chapel Hill.

Susan Lefler's poems have appeared in journals including *Pinesong, Asheville Poetry Review, Main Street Rag, Pembroke Review, Pisgah Review, North Carolina Literary Review,* and in the anthologies *Gutters and Alleyways, Kakalak, What Matters, ... and love....* Her first poetry collection *Rendering the Bones* was published in 2011 by Wind Press. She was nominated in 2014 for a Pushcart Prize. She is from Brevard and is studying for an MFA in Poetry at Queens University of Charlotte.

Stephanie Levin received her MFA in Poetry from the University of Virginia and her MA in Literature & Writing from Hollins University. Her work has appeared in *Green Mountains Review, Folio, River Styx, Prairie Schooner,* and *Shenandoah Smoke of Her Body* was chosen by Dorianne Laux as winner of the 2011 Jacar Press Poetry Book Prize.

Diane Lockward is the author of *The Crafty Poet: A Portable Workshop* and three poetry books, *Temptation by Water, What Feeds Us,* and *Eve's Red Dress.* Her poems have been included in such journals as *Harvard Review, Southern Poetry Review,* and *Prairie Schooner.* Her work has also been featured on *Poetry Daily, Verse Daily,* and *The Writer's Almanac.*

A native Midwesterner, **Christina Lovin** now makes her home in Central Kentucky, where she teaches writing at Eastern Kentucky University. She has published five volumes of poetry: *Echo, A Stirring in the Dark, Flesh, Little Fires,* and *What We Burned for Warmth.* Her writing is widely published in journals and anthologies. "Scars" was published online in Levure Littéraire and in print in the *Naugatuck River Review.*

Twice winner of the annual Brockman-Campbell Award, **Peter Makuck** lives on Bogue Banks. He has authored five volumes of poetry, most recently *Long Lens: New & Selected Poems* (BOA Editions, Ltd), which was nominated for a Pulitzer Prize. Forthcoming in September 2016 from BOA is *Mandatory Evacuation.* Syracuse University Press published his third collection of short stories, *Allegiance and Betrayal.* His essays and reviews, poems and stories have appeared in *The Hudson Review, North American Review, Southern Poetry Review,* and *The Sewanee Review.* Founder and editor of *Tar River Poetry* from 1978 to 2006, Makuck is a Distinguished Professor Emeritus at East Carolina University.

Shahé Mankerian's most recent manuscript, *History of Forgetfulness*, has been a finalist at four prestigious competitions: the 2013 Crab Orchard Series in Poetry Open Competition, the 2013 Bibby First Book Competition, the Quercus Review Press Fall Poetry Book Award 2013, and the 2014 White Pine Press Poetry Prize. His poems have appeared in *Mizna.*

Sharon Fagan McDermott is a poet and teacher based in Pittsburgh, PA. She has three chapbooks of poetry: *Voluptuous* (Ultima Obscura Press); *Alley Scatting* (Parallel Press); and *Bitter Acoustic*, chosen by poet Betty Adcock as the winner of Jacar Press 2011 chapbook competition.

Michael McFee has taught poetry writing at UNC-Chapel Hill for 25 years. The author of fourteen books, most recently *That Was Oasis* (Carnegie Mellon University Press, 2012), he received the 2009 James Still Award for Writing about the Appalachian South, from the Fellowship of Southern Writers.

Susan Laughter Meyers won the Cider Press Review Editors' Prize for her latest collection, *My Dear, Dear Stagger Grass*. Her earlier book, *Keep and Give Away* (University of South Carolina Press), won the South Carolina Poetry Book Prize. She and her husband Blue live in rural Givhans, South Carolina. "Oconee" was the Artist-in-Residence poem for the SC State Park System.

Kelly Michels grew up in Virginia Beach and received her MFA from North Carolina State University. Her poems have appeared in *Best New Poets, Green Mountains Review, Ruminate, Blue Fifth Review, Nimrod, Redivider, Reed Magazine, One*, and others.

Devon Miller-Duggan has published poems in *Rattle, Shenandoah, Margie, Christianity and Literature, Gargoyle*. She teaches Creative Writing at the University of Delaware. Her books include *Pinning the Bird to the Wall* from Tres Chicas Books in 2008 and a chapbook of poems about angels, *Neither Prayer, Nor Bird* from Finishing Line Press in 2013.

A professor at the University of North Carolina School of the Arts, **Joseph Mills** holds an endowed chair, the Susan Burress Wall Distinguished Professorship in the Humanities. He has published five collections of poetry, most recently *Angels, Thieves and Winemakers* (2nd edition), and *This Miraculous Turning*.

Nancy Carol Moody is the author of *Photograph with Girls* (Traprock Books), and her poetry has appeared in *The Southern Review, Phoebe, The Los Angeles Review* and *Nimrod*. She lives in Eugene, Oregon.

Ruth Moose was on the Creative Writing faculty at UNC-Chapel Hill for 15 years. Her first novel, *Doing it at the Dixie Dew*, was published by St. Martin's Press in 2014. Previously published are three collections of short stories, *The Wreath Ribbon Quilt, Dreaming in Color*, and *Neighbors and Other Strangers*, with individual stories in *The Atlantic* and other places, and six collections of poetry, most recently, *The Librarian and Other Poems*. She's received a MacDowell Fellowship and a Chapman Fellowship for Teaching. She lives in Pittsboro, NC.

Thylias Moss is Professor Emerita from the University of Michigan, Department of English and School of Art & Design. She has published ten books, most recently, *Tokyo Butter(2006) and Slave Moth* (2004). She has twice been a finalist in the National Book Critics Circle Award: *Last Chance for the Tarzan Holler* and *Pyramid of Bone*. She is a "limited forker" and developed "limited fork theory" as a way to make stuff, share stuff, think stuff, and be stuff, as systems of interaction that allow everything to fork and connect on some scale, in some location, for some duration —connection is most vital, as no one "owns" the many forms of existence! Forthcoming in 2016, is a volume of new and selected poetry from Persea Books.

Leanne O'Sullivan was born in 1983 and comes from the Beara Peninsula in West Cork, Ireland. She has won several awards including the Rooney Prize for Irish Literature. She has published three collections of poetry, *Waiting for My Clothes* (2004), *Cailleach: The Hag of Beara* (2009), and *The Mining Road* (2013). She is currently Writer-in-Residence at University College, Cork.

Alan Michael Parker is the author of eight books of poetry, including *The Ladder* (Tupelo 2016), three novels, and editor of four other works. His awards include three Pushcart Prizes, inclusion in *Best American Poetry* 2011 and 2015, and the NC Book Award. Douglas C. Houchens Professor of English at Davidson College, he also teaches in the University of Tampa low residency MFA program.

Deborah Pope has published three books—*Fanatic Heart, Mortal World* and *Falling Out of the Sky* —from LSU Press. Her work has appeared in the journals *Threepenny Review, Poetry, Southern Review, Southwest Quarterly, Poetry Northwest*, among others.

Dannye Romine Powell's fourth collection, *Nobody Calls Me Darling Anymore*, will be published by Press 53 in the fall of 2015. She is a two-time winner of the Brockman-Campbell Award and a recipient of fellowships from the NEA and the NC Arts Council. She lives in Charlotte, NC.

David Radavich has published seven volumes of poetry, most recently *The Countries We Live In* (2014). His plays have been performed across the U.S., including six Off-Off-Broadway, and in Europe. He is the current president of the North Carolina Poetry Society.

Shannon Rayne is a Vancouver-based writer completing her MFA in Creative Writing at the University of British Columbia. Her poems appear in *Live from the Centre*, an anthology of West Coast poets, *Filling Station, Room* and *Poetry Is Dead*. She`s compiling a manuscript about coffee culture through the lens of poetry.

Susan Rich is the author of four books, including *Cloud Pharmacy* (a runner-up for the Julie Suk Award) and *The Alchemist's Kitchen*. She co-edited *The Strangest of Theatres: Poets Writing Across Borders* with Brian Turner, and has received awards from The Times Literary Supplement and the Fulbright Foundation. Rich's individual poems appear in *Prairie Schooner, New England Review*, and *World Literature Today*.

Rachel Richardson has received fellowships from the National Endowment for the Arts, Sewanee Writers' Conference, and Stegner Program at Stanford University. She is the author of *Copperhead* (2011) and *Hundred-Year Wave* (forthcoming 2016), both from Carnegie Mellon University Press. Recent poems appear in *New England Review, Birmingham Poetry Review,*and *Memorious*.

Linwood Rumney's poetry has appeared in *Crab Orchard Review*, *North American Review*, *Puerto del Sol*, *Southern Review*, and elsewhere. This poem was originally published in the Winter 2013-2014 issue of *Ploughshares*.

Nora Shepard received an MFA in poetry from North Carolina State University in 2005 under the direction of John Balaban and a second MFA from the Warren Wilson Program for Writers. She teaches creative writing and poetry at NCSU. She has poems recently published in *Poet Lore's 125th Anniversary Issue, Great River Review*, and forthcoming in *Cortland Review*.

Martha Silano is the author of *Reckless Lovely, The Little Office of the Immaculate Conception, Blue Positive, What the Truth Tastes Like*, and, with Kelli Russell Agodon, *The Daily Poet: Day-By-Day Prompts for Your Writing Practice*. Martha edits *Crab Creek Review* and teaches at Bellevue College.

Anya Silver has three books published or forthcoming from the Louisiana State University Press: *From Nothing* (2016), *I Watched You Disappear* (2014), and *The Ninety-Third Name of God* (2010). She was awarded Georgia Author of the Year in poetry for *I Watched You Disappear* in 2015, and has been featured by Garrison Keillor on *The Writer's Almanac* and by Ted Kooser in his syndicated column, *American Lives in Poetry*. She has also been published widely in literary journals. She is Professor of English at Mercer University and lives with her husband and son in downtown Macon, Georgia.

Karen Skolfield's book *Frost in the Low Areas* won the 2014 PEN New England Award in poetry. New poems appear in *Baltimore Review, Crab Orchard Review, Indiana Review, One, Pleiades*, and others; she teaches writing to engineers at the University of Massachusetts Amherst.

Noel Sloboda's poetry has recently appeared in *Bayou, Fourteen Hills, PANK*, and *Weave*. He is the author of the poetry collections *Shell Games* (sunnyoutside, 2008) and *Our Rarer Monsters* (sunnyoutside, 2013) as well as several chapbooks. He teaches at Penn State York.

Katherine Soniat's seventh collection, *Bright Stranger,* is forthcoming from Louisiana State University Press, spring 2016. *The Swing Girl* (LSU Press) was selected as Best Collection of 2011 by the Poetry Council of North Carolina. A chapbook, *The Goodbye Animals,* recently received the Turtle Island Quarterly Award and *A Shared Life* won The Iowa Poetry Prize (University of Iowa Press).

Marjorie Stelmach's fourth volume of poems is *Without Angels* (Mayapple). Previous volumes include *A History of Disappearance* and *Bent upon Light* (Tampa). Recent work has appeared or is forthcoming in *Boulevard, Cincinnati Review, Gettysburg Review, New Letters & Prairie Schooner.* She lives in St. Louis, Missouri.

Shelby Stephenson's recent books are *Steal Away* (Jacar Press) and the reprint of *Fiddledeedee* (Press 53). He is North Carolina's current Poet Laureate. He was professor of English and editor of *Pembroke Magazine* until his retirement in 2010.

Julie Suk is the author of six volumes of poetry, including the forthcoming *Astonished to Wake* (Jacar Press 2016). Others include *Lie Down With Me: New and Selected Poems* (Autumn House Press 2011), *The Dark Takes Aim*, and *The Angel of Obsession*. Her work appears in *Cimarron Review, The Midwest Quarterly, One, Southern Poetry Review,* and others.

Marilyn L. Taylor, former Poet Laureate of Wisconsin (2009 - 2010) and of Milwaukee (2004 - 2005), has published six collections of poetry. Her award-winning work has appeared in many anthologies and journals, including *Poetry, American Scholar,* and *Measure*. Marilyn's column on craft appeared bi-monthly for five years in *The Writer* magazine.

Lee Colin Thomas lives and writes in Minneapolis. His work has been selected for a Loft Mentor Series Award in poetry and an honorable mention for the Minnesota Emerging Writers Grant. Lee's poems have appeared in *Poet Lore, Salamander, The Gay and Lesbian Review Worldwide, Water ~ Stone Review*, and elsewhere.

Raised in Oklahoma, **Anna Weaver** lives in North Carolina with her two daughters. Her poems have appeared in print and online journals, anthologies, public art projects, and once on a postcard. A self-described open mic tourist, she has performed in eight states and the District of Columbia.

Diana Whitney's first book, *Wanting It,* became an indie poetry bestseller. Her writing has appeared in *The Boston Globe, The San Francisco Chronicle, The Rumpus, Crab Orchard Review,* and many more. Diana blogs about the darker side of motherhood for *The Huffington Post* and runs a yoga studio in Vermont.

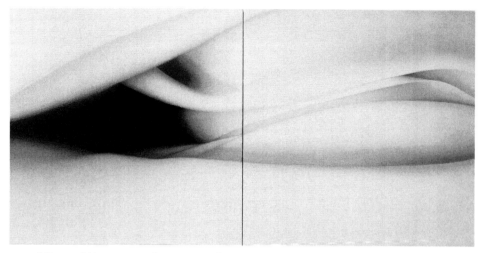

Alison Watt was born in Greenock in 1965 and studied at Glasgow School of Art. In 1987 she won the National Portrait Gallery's coveted annual award and in the late 1980s and early 90s she became well known for her paintings of figures, often female nudes. Watt's exhibition *Fold* in 1997 at Edinburgh's Fruitmarket Gallery marked a turning point by introducing fabric alongside these figures. This was followed by *Shift* in 2000, her solo exhibition at the Scottish National Gallery of Modern Art, which saw Watt move away from the figure and display a series of twelve large works depicting swathes of fabric.

Watt's residency as Associate Artist at The National Gallery, London culminated in the landmark solo exhibition *Phantom* in 2008. She was awarded an Order of the British Empire in the same year. Recent exhibitions include *Dark Light,* Ingleby Gallery, Edinburgh and *Pier Art Gallery,* Orkney (2007); *Autoriatratto,* Uffizi Gallery (2010), Italy; *Reflecting Glenfiddich,* The Fleming Collection, London (2011) and *Hiding in Full View,* Ingleby Gallery (2011).

In 2014, as part of the Nationwide *GENERATION* programme of exhibitions, a retrospective exhibition of Watt's paintings was held at Perth Museum and Art Gallery, and a solo display was presented at the Scottish National Gallery of Modern Art, Edinburgh. Watt was recently commissioned to design a large scale tapestry – *Butterfly* – in collaboration with Dovecot studios and Scottish Opera which was installed in Theatre Royal, Glasgow. Watt's paintings were recently exhibited as part of the major group exhibition *Reality: Modern & Contemporary British Painting* at the Sainsbury Centre for Visual Arts, Norwich which tours to the Walker Art Gallery, Liverpool in July 2015.